WHAT A WAY TO RUN A RAILROAD

AN ANALYSIS OF RADICAL FAILURE

by Charles Landry, Dave Morley, Russell Southwood, Patrick Wright

Comedia Publishing Group
9 Poland Street, London W1V 3DG   Tel: 01-439 2059

Organizations and Democracy –

This new series is concerned with questions of management as they apply to campaigning and voluntary organizations and also to the various movements of social change. Some books will attempt to define the existing range of self managed activity, while others will discuss and publicise ways of working that are both effective and congruent with democratic aspirations and principles.

Too often democracy and self management have meant inertia and inaction. While the series opposes the blind extension of management ideas into organizations with social goals it considers that worthy incompetence needs to be overcome. Series editor Patrick Wright is currently head of the Management Development Unit at the National Council for Voluntary Organisations.

First published in 1985 by Comedia Publishing Group
9 Poland Street, London W1 3DG.

© Comedia Publishing Group

ISBN 0-906890-80-2

British Library Cataloguing in Publication Data
What a way to run a railroad: an analysis of radical failure
1. Social group work – Great Britain
2. Community organisation – Great Britain
I. Landry, Charles
361.8′0941 HV245

Typeset by Photosetting, 6 Foundry House, Stars Lane, Yeovil, Somerset
BA20 1NL. Tel: 0935 23684

Printed in Great Britain by
Unwin Brothers Ltd.,
The Gresham Press, Old Woking, Surrey

Trade Distribution by
Comedia, 9 Poland Street, London W1

Contents

Acknowledgements

We would like to acknowledge the following people who were influential, for good or ill, in forming our thinking on the issues discussed in this book.

Diane Abbot
Nick Anning
Amanda Baird
Chaz Ball
Dave Berry
Jonathon Bloch
Peter Brinson
Charlotte Brunsdon
Tony Bunyan
Tom Burke
Nadine Cartner
Gail Chester
Dave Clark
Derek Cohen
Mike Cooley
Liz Cooper
Tony Eccles
Michael Edwards
Frank Elston
Paddy French
Chris Farley
Federation of Worker Writers
Federation of Radical Booksellers
Sue Field Reid
Nicholas Garnham
John Goodman
Ted Goodman
Tim Gopsill
Stuart Hall
Bernard Halloran

Frances Haste
Sylvia Harvey
Charlie Harness
Tarek Hassan
Chris Hutton
Cherill Hicks
Anthony Hirst
Steve Horigan
Terry Illot
Pam Isherwood
Mike Jempson
Dorothy Jones
Phil Kelly
John Knepler
Richard Lapper
Imogen Mark
Kathy Myers
H. O. Nazareth
Tony Nichols
Alec Nove
Robert Oakeshott
Frank Parkin
Simon Partridge
Stef Pixner
Mike Prest
Rod Prince
Radical Publications Group
Joanna Rollo
Christopher Roper
Sheila Rowbotham

John Rowley
Amon Saba Saakana
Rose Shapiro
Robert Skidelsky
Graham Smith
Keith Smith
Raul Sohr
Judith Stone
Dave Taylor
Peter Thompson

Valerie and Sylvia Tomlin
Jim Tomlinson
Moira Turnbull
Brian Wade
Ian Walker
Paul Westlake
Brian Whitaker
Chris Whitbread
Ken Worpole
Bob Young

Also, finally, a big thanks to Micropro's programme, Wordstar.

'If only I knew how to start some kind of business! My dear friend, all theory is dismal and only business flourishes. Unfortunately I have learnt this too late.'   *Marx to Engels (1862)*

Introduction

This short book is written on the basis of our experiences of working in the alternative/radical press, in publishing, in libertarian and community politics, and in the voluntary sector over the last ten years. This experience has included work with community newspapers and magazines as well as with a variety of distribution and publication projects as well as work for other kinds of radical projects. We take, on the whole, a doleful view of this recent history, but our reasons for exhuming it are positive.

Our aim is to define certain factors which, in our view, help to account for the collapse and failure of many radical projects in this sector. We offer this analysis of 'past failures' in the hope that other people – whether they agree or disagree with our specific analysis – will recognize many of the problems discussed here and feel it worthwhile to consider and discuss them further.

Let us start with a catalogue of the relevant failures. Among the radical organizations and publications which have closed down or disintegrated into inactivity over the last few years are: Achilles Heel, Agitprop, Anarchist Library, Anarchist Workers Association, Anticircus, The Beast, Beautiful Stranger, Bethnal Rouge, Black Liberator, Black Phoenix, Bogus Books, Brixton Boss, Case Con, Captain Swing, Cinema Rising, Crann Tara, Creative Mind, December 6th Group, East London Gay Liberation Front, Educational Libertarian Network Enough, Fightback, Freewheeling, Gay Left, Humpty Dumpty, Index Books, Inside Story, Islington Socialist Club, LASH, Last Exit, The Left Centre, The Leveller, Libertarian Education, Lunatic Fringe, MS Print, Musics, Nell/Ned Gate, News from Neasden, News Release, On Yer Bike, Orwell Books, Outcome, Penny Black, Peoples News Service, Prompt, Radical Education, Red Rag, Rising Free, Fourth Idea, Scarlet Woman, SCARP, Seeds, Shrew, Slate, Solidarity for Social Revolution, South London Socialist Club, Spice Island, Spinster, Stage One, State Research, Temporary Hoarding, Toolshed, Teachers Action, Ultima Thule, Unemployed Workers Union, Up Against the Law, Undercurrents,

Voices, Wedge, Whole Earth, Wild Cat, Womens Action, Women in Action, Womens Liberation Workshop, Womens Report, Xtra, Zero, Zig, and, in addition, innumerable community newspapers in different parts of the country.

With a few brave exceptions, where there was once the promise of a network of properly independent publications and organizations developing and expressing a diversity of public activity and thinking, we now find only the Fleet Street monopolies.

It's true that every publication and organization has its day, and success or failure cannot be measured merely in terms of how long a project survives. Closure need not, of itself, indicate failure – sometimes it's just time to call it a day, when the job is done. It is also true that many of these publications and organizations were ludicrously under-resourced in relation to the scale of the issues with which they were trying to grapple. But while mitigating factors exist, we do not think that the collapse of these publications and organizations can be dismissed as something of which they themselves were entirely innocent.

Although we are talking about failure, we are not interested in allocating blame or pointing fingers of personal accusation. With the exception of a detailed study of the situation on *The Leveller* of which we have personal experience (see Chapter II), we have made our arguments without reference to extensive examples, since we wish to avoid getting bogged down in squabbles over exact details: who said what, when and so forth.

We know how difficult it is to sustain a critical and oppositional project in a society which is structured at all levels against it. But these external difficulties do not themselves provide a sufficient explanation. Some radical organizations appear to believe that failure in a capitalist world is a direct sign of 'correctness' – capitalism proved evil once again. Such are the pure but vicious delights of ideological piety. There's no success like failure, as someone famous once said.

In short, we develop our arguments with two purposes:

- To analyse and explain the reasons why a number of the libertarian projects which emerged in the 1970s ultimately failed.

- To offer, on the basis of this analysis, some positive proposals as to how the problems of organization, management and finance within radical projects might be better tackled in the future.

Finally, questions of organization and management are now also being discussed with a new intensity within the women's and black movement. We cannot speak for this experience but we hope to include writings from these constituencies in future titles of the series.

Chapter I

History and Ideology

Introduction

Perhaps it seems strange, now that libertarianism is no longer a serious political force, to devote our energies to analysing its failures. But we feel such an analysis to be timely because we believe that libertarian culture was not only an important item on the political agenda of the 1970s but that the perspectives of this culture continue to influence many of today's radical organizations.

While we would argue that the culture was more influential than its adherents, it is still worth noting that many of those involved in the failed libertarian projects of the 1970s have now moved into positions of power (not least in local government, community work and the Labour Party). Many of the key figures in the squatting networks, women's groups and community projects of the 1970s are now employed as planning officers, researchers, advisers and information officers, or as executives of powerful public bodies with large budgets. In this journey to the foothills of power, they have carried into these institutions many of the ideological perspectives and premises established in their politically formative years: a particular set of libertarian attitudes to power, organization, democracy, economics and culture. This libertarian culture was an important component of the 'moral energy' behind Tony Benn's attempt in 1981 to become Deputy Leader of the Labour Party. Many of Tony Benn's now widely known views on democracy and many other issues stem from his embracing the ideas that libertarians carried with them into the Labour Party, and his becoming the 'representative' of this culture within the forum of parliamentary politics.

The days after

As the left and many of its projects have recently seemed to collapse about our ears we would hope to be excused for posing some questions about the origin of the libertarian political perspective which we see as still dominant in the radical movement.

Could it be that we can't solve the political equations we're all still puzzling over because we're using the wrong kind of algebra? This is a particularly difficult question to get to grips with, given that one of the factors in the libertarian equation is a commitment to informality, which means that nowhere is this 'political algebra' laid out. It is a particularly hidden agenda, which influences, for instance, that set of assumptions about the meaning of 'equality' or 'democracy' – assumptions so common that they don't seem to need to be spelt out explicitly. These unquestioned (and, for some, still unquestionable) assumptions define the limits of our political debates. However, if the algebra is at fault it's no good expecting to be able to solve any further equations with it, and we may therefore have to start by attempting to make that 'hidden agenda' explicit in order to examine its terms more clearly.

Over the last few years (and certainly since the 1979 election) the right has resumed its dominance in British political life in direct contrast to the experience of the 1960s and 1970s, when in many areas of life, the left had defined the issues to which the right was forced to respond. One can, of course, point to some more hopeful signs of life – such as the attempts within the Labour Party to recover from its electoral decimation by recognizing just how much is wrong with the party, the level of popular support for the campaigns to save the Metropolitan Authorities, etc. But, as yet, these are relatively isolated 'moments' of (relative) success – within a framework set by the right.

In general terms our argument here can be linked to Stuart Hall's analysis of Thatcherism. Contrary to the (perhaps deliberately erroneous) claims of recent critics like Tony Benn, Hall has never argued that 'Thatcherism' is a cult centred on the supposedly charismatic personality of Margaret Thatcher. Since before the 1979 election he has aimed to track and define the extent to which Thatcher has succeeded in gaining real popular support for the cultural project which is so central to her version of Neo-Conservatism. His point is that we need to understand the *real* (rather than merely 'ideological') basis of support that this political strategy has achieved at the level of popular perception and self-understanding.[1] While Thatcher's statements about, say, 'rolling back the frontiers of the state' strike a genuine chord for many working-class people, the opposed 'vision' of a desirable society developed by the left through the 1970s has largely failed to win any comparable form of popular support.

If we are to have any hope of winning that support, rather than simply blaming the mis-representations of the media, we should look at what is in fact wrong with the 'vision' and be prepared to change and develop it. The rate of failure and attrition amongst radical projects has been unacceptably high. An analysis of why this is the case will involve us in a little bit of time-travelling, to see where difficulties have come from. For one thing we need to understand which were the problems for which libertarianism seemed to provide some kind of solution, and what it means today to be trying to ride a bike which seems to have square wheels. The key question is how many of the difficulties which we currently face are self-imposed: after all, didn't we design the square wheels in the first place? To take but two examples, how did we ever get into the situation where, in a community bookshop which needs to sell a certain quantity of books in a given week to have any chance of survival (let alone any chance of independent survival without complete financial dependence on state subsidy), a male worker takes out of its display-window the copies of *Lace* because they are selling too well, against the wishes of the female worker in the shop, who doesn't feel that her feminism is threatened by the sale of titles of this kind? Or again, what do we do in a situation where the workers in a project have to pay interest on money they borrow from the bank to sustain their work, but are unwilling 'on principle' to put any monies received into an interest-earning account? How, under the conditions set by these kinds of self-imposed roadblocks, can we have any hope of developing an outgoing and ambitious political movement? And so, backwards into the murky depths of recent history, in search of explanations for these difficulties.

A history of blind spots

We believe that there were fundamental and characteristic weaknesses in the political culture of the oppositional movements of the 1970s, and that these blind spots resulted over and again in a set of predispositions which made failure all the more likely.

What, then, do we mean by the political culture of the 1970s? We are focusing on an oppositional culture created and experienced by the generation which grew up during the long post-war boom of the late fifties and early sixties. Consumerism; affluence; the supposedly 'post-industrial'/'post-class'/'post-scarcity'/society; the 'end of ideology'; such were the terms of the understanding which influenced this generation. People had been told that they had never had it so good, and in some senses this was true enough. The welfare state was in its heyday, having been expanded to provide a net through which it was more difficult to fall than in previous times. Similarly, the growth of the education system had provided many people with new spaces – for dreaming and drifting, certainly, but also for more critical analysis and the development of new perspectives.

By 1968 a broad 'alternative' counter-culture had developed, inspired not least by innovations in the arts and new mass cultural forms. This movement was as romantic as it was political, hence its narcissisms and its interest in 'alternative' or communal lifestyles. Its hedonism was partly drug-based (as were significant parts of its economy), and its ideal of freedom was to a large extent understood in sexual terms, although the male-orientated terms of this sexuality were scarcely questioned at the time.

The traditional political opposition, from the Labour Party through to the Communist Party, was unable to take on the issues which these new movements posed. With the 'events' of May 1968 and the growing opposition to the Vietnam War, the New Left as it is now known came into being. This was the moment of Trotskyism (which was itself no part of the mainstream) and of 'democratic centralism' against which the women's movement especially soon came to express its own demands.

Thus began the politicization of everyday life. This was not just a matter of redefining political domination in new areas like health, sexual relations, and education. The day of the fully occupied or total activist had also dawned. It became obligatory to wake up active and move through a day of committed childcare, politicised teaching in a polytechnic or college of further education, a union meeting at lunchtime, a support group and campaign meeting in the afternoon, an early evening meeting at a radical project, and the final exhausted collapse into a collective house meeting to round it all off. Of course, the one thing that such a lifestyle could be guaranteed to produce was a strong sense of self-righteousness. If one lived such a testing and fully committed life, surely (a) one was entitled to political success and (b) no one who 'failed' this strenuous course could be accepted as an equal. This perspective often quickly turned from self-righteousness into moralism and even zealotry.

The fabric of oppositional life in the sixties and early seventies was developed in a context where scarcity, in any of its economic, ecological or social guises was far from prominent on the political agenda. The oil crisis had not occurred. It was still possible to feel that there was 'enough to go round' and thus 'enough' to allow all sorts of utopian dreams to come to pass. If there were problems, therefore, these were to do with affluence – with the behaviour of those with too much. The problem in focus was that of distributive justice alone – i.e. how existing wealth ought to be divided up. While this is obviously a key issue for any socialist perspective, it makes no sense to consider this issue without attention to its necessary complement – how is wealth to be produced. Such were the luxuries of the West, before the oil-crisis of the mid-70s, that this second question was largely obscured.

The problem has been that many of those on the left have carried this monocular perspective (in which the problem of wealth-creation is not addressed, other than gesturally) through into the quite different conditions of the present period. Again, the contrast with Thatcherism is instructive: while its proposed 'solutions' to the problem of wealth creation may be abhorrent, it did address this question centrally. No political perspective which fails to do that, and which indeed fails to come up with better practical solutions to that problem, can have any hope of success under present conditions.

In this age of 'lifestyle politics', problems tended to be posed in psychological, therapeutic and communal terms. This, after all, was the generation which became fascinated by ideas of *cultural* revolution rather than more prosaic questions of political economy. In this situation the idea of *equality* could come to the fore, not understood as a matter of equality before the law, or of equality of opportunity, but instead interpreted and revalued in terms of *sharing* – thus the emphasis on the collective, and on communal lifestyles. There was a vague romanticisation of the cultural revolution in China, together with something more particular that came from this same source: a stress on the need for (and the possibility of) overcoming the division of mental from manual labour. This perspective was rarely developed beyond the level of being a kind of agrarian fantasy, which even if it always seemed a rather quaint and exotic bird as it flew through the inner cities of twentieth century Western Europe, went well with a strongly anti-capitalist and also somewhat Pre-Raphaelite orientation. The idea seems, indeed, to have been *everyone* sharing *everything* voluntarily, *everyone* developing *all* human capacities.[2] Thus, while the 'haves' of the affluent society were certainly opposed, the challenge was not made just from the point of view of the 'have-nots', but also from the perspective of an authenticity of 'being'. The personal, as everyone (and not just the male honchos of vanguardist parties) heard, was political.

Many of the people involved in these movements were disaffected members of the middle class, whose main way of feeling solidarity with the oppressed seems to have been achieved through the deliberate adoption of an 'oppressed' lifestyle. They literally dragged themselves down to a level where they were consciously self-oppressed (particularly in the monetary sense, as they chose to exploit themselves financially, often working very long hours for little or no pay). As Lyn Segal put it: 'We supported those most oppressed ... and believed you could only fight back if you shared the material situation of the most oppressed ...'[3]

The squatting/dole nexus became a moral imperative. If you wanted a home, squatting was the first option considered, followed by council housing, which also was 'good'; renting was suffering, and buying was bourgeois. The same moralistic judgements were made over money. Everything was dragged down to the worst possible level – so, being poor was seen as in itself good (or 'pure' – with all the Christian overtones of that terminology) while wanting more was bad; and by living in self-imposed poverty one was (magically) allied to the working class, the Third World, etc. The predominant model of politics here was that you could only base views or actions on feeling as dreadful as those you claimed to represent. The problem though, as Lyn Segal again points out, is that 'Misery does not always equal militancy, and those worst oppressed are sometimes so smashed that it's hard for them to fight back at all'

The impact of feminism

In the mid-1970s feminism made a major impact on political debate on the left, redefining the agenda of politics, and setting the criteria of decision making. Feminism was the one political perspective that had not been discredited, and had something to say about the areas of political activity which had just been opened up through the politicization of lifestyle politics. At the same time a particular set of notions about direct action, non-hierarchical organization, even 'anti-organization' became dominant, and they had nothing necessarily to do with feminism. The reason why these perspectives came in through the side door, once feminists had forced it open, was that they were compatible (in a way that other traditions of organized politics were not) with the political criteria established by feminism. What was important was the way the agenda of issues was set, and the way that agenda set definite limits to the range of politically 'acceptable' activities/questions/lifestyles.

For the sake of clarity, we can try to express some part of this process by way of the following caricature of the chain of events. Firstly, feminism supplied criteria of adequacy which only particular libertarian/anarchist political traditions could fulfil. Secondly, these political traditions themselves led in particular directions: they had few working class traditions/connections and few trade union connections, so the field of workplace politics was excluded. Thirdly, they were not concerned with electoral politics, so that went by the board. They were into direct action, and that often led to a short-term politics of tactics over strategy, excluding any idea of long-term planning. What this led to, of course, was community politics or direct action. Once the trade union connection is excluded the workplace is off-limits and there is only the community to work in. Community politics often meant short-term direct action on limited objectives involving an often incoherent set of contradictory demands from different sectional interests within 'the community'.

The central absence here is a sense of long-term strategy – which is perhaps the key blind spot in the libertarian perspective. As Sheila Rowbotham[4] put it: 'what of the strategic consequences of action? Libertarians seemed to dismiss these.' Long-term strategic questions (such as 'the need for investment', in the sense of provision for replacement of personnel; taking care to avoid 'building on sand', in the sense of avoiding setting up structures which will generate organizational 'burn-out' by relying on intense self-exploitation, etc.) – none of these issues could even be *thought* through within the set of terms provided by the libertarian political algebra of the time. The conceptual space in which these things could appear as important issues did not exist. Looking back at that history, it is possible now to identify some of the reasons why these things got shoved off the agenda. What we have to do now is find ways to rewrite that agenda, because otherwise the same flawed perspectives will continue to dominate the politics of the present. To paraphrase another famous observation, if we fail to understand our own failures we will be doomed to repeat them.

This sketch is patchy enough, but it must do. The main point is that by 1974 – with the oil crisis and the miners' strike – the conditions had changed. This is not to say that the dream didn't go on, sometimes in plainly bizarre and florid forms. As the general economic climate worsened, a new form of subsidy was found in the gift of the local apparatus of the various left labour administrations, which funded – directly and indirectly – many of the organizations and projects through which this political culture moved forward. While things certainly changed, and there was no direct continuity with the sixties, some things carried through. Among them was a double, although often far from 'dialectical' definition of politics – as a matter of personal *being* as well as *action*. When it works well this connection can be rich indeed, but it can take disastrous and destructive forms as well.

The revolt against structure

An essential feature of the political culture of the 1970s was its rejection of formal, bureaucratic structures in favour of loose-knit informal networks. This replacement of one type of organization by another was of central importance, given that the emphasis at the time was as much on *how* things were to be done as on *what* was to be done.

The belief in the importance of non-hierarchical structures and 'networking' was strongly influenced by the women's movement and by the forms of organization, such as the consciousness-raising groups, which that movement had generated.

In 1974 the Anarchist Workers' Association circulated a reprint of an article written by Jo Freeman, titled 'The Tyranny of Structurelessness'. At the time the ideas expressed in it did not receive the attention they deserved. Freeman, an American feminist, had questioned the possibility of 'getting rid of structure'. She argued that there is no such thing as a 'structureless' group – the only question is what kind of structure a group has. In essence, she argued, the libertarian reaction against the Stalinism of 'centralist' organizations and the libertarian movement's concern to prevent leaders of a hierarchical organization accumulating power, had led up a blind alley. The 'old' structures were not being abolished: they were simply obscured within informal organizational structures.

Freeman's argument was that the exercise of power is inevitable – the point is how to control it; how to make those who held power accountable: 'If the movement continues to deliberately *not* select who shall exercise power, it does not thereby abolish power. All it does is to abdicate the right to demand that those who do exercise power and influence, be responsible for it . . . When informal elites are combined with a myth of "structurelessness" there can be no attempt to put limits on the use of power.'

The problem is that informal elites are not accountable to anyone. Because their power has no explicit basis there are no straightforward mechanisms for removing their influence. Unless you are part of the influential group it is hard to know who has real power in an organization run by an informal elite: who you should lobby for what purpose; what are the criteria on which decisions are based; which of the organization's goals should take priority. Decisions will still be taken, agendas set and issues resolved, in any informal organization, but the basis on which these decisions are made is simply not made explicit.

Entry to the elite can be hard. Those who do not fit – because of class, race, sexual preference or politics – will be discouraged from becoming part of the 'inner circle'. Those who are part of that elite inevitably have personal and political interests in maintaining the status quo. The consequence is usually that groups of friends become the main means of organizational activity. Crucial discussions are held, and crucial decisions made in the pub, or in someone's front room. The perpetuation of the elite is institutionalized and becomes very hard to break.

The attempt to do without structure only prevents the formulation of *formal* structures. Structures are inevitable. All groups have *informal* structures; some groups also have *formal* structures. In those with only informal structures power relations are masked and the rules of power (how and why decisions are taken, for instance) are known only to the members of the informal elite. There is, therefore, no explicit mechanism for addressing the problems produced by the informal wielding of power. Many of these problems derive from transferring the structure of the consciousness-raising group to other spheres of activity. Unstructured groups, although ideal for getting people to talk about their lives, are not the most effective form for getting things done. And the less structure a movement has, the less control it has over the direction in which it develops.

Many of these issues were addressed by Sheila Rowbotham in an essay titled 'The Women's Movement and Organizing for Socialism' published in *Beyond the Fragment* in 1977/78. As Rowbotham put it, reflecting on the libertarian movement of the early 1970s: 'The stress was on learning through doing, and on the need for experience to be the source of theory. Your politics were connected in what you did and *how* you did it ... the attack against capitalist society should carry the future within the present. Thus there should be no hierarchy, no elites, no chair, no committees, no speakers, and even no meetings in some cases. Or the meetings emerged into and became life; and life thus became meetings!'[5]

This libertarian perspective had a number of defects, chief of which was the problem that the breaking down of hierarchy and denying of skills led to an inturned, moralistic and exclusive network. Rowbotham recognized that a lack of structure could make it difficult for women to join particular social networks and could lead to cliqueishness, thus becoming undemocratic. Participatory democracy also had its problems: 'The problems about participatory democracy are evident. If you are not able to be present you can't participate. Whoever turns up next time can reverse the previous decision. If very few people turn up they are lumbered with the responsibility. It is a very open situation, and anyone with a gift for either emotional blackmail or a conviction of the need to intervene can do so without being checked by any accepted procedure'

The following account of working in a collective, comes from Richard Seyd, a member of the Red Ladder Theatre collective in the mid-1970s. Seyd graphically illustrates the extent to which a totally open structure can lead to manipulation through hidden power relations:[6]

'Essentially, the group was structured so that every decision, however small, needed the unanimous agreement of every individual on it before it could be acted upon. Of course, in theory, this seems the perfect democratic approach. In practice it meant that those with the strongest personalities (the more pushy ones) dominated the group. Through the course of an argument, those in a minority would eventually put up their hands and make the decision unanimous even when they did not agree with it, just so that work could continue. This method of working itself created personality antagonisms, and often reduced arguments to the level of personality differences. When resentments built up to an intolerable level, explosions occurred, and often we would sit down for days in order to work out the problems. Because we believed there could be nothing wrong with the structure, since it was so democratic, this working-out led us into people's individual personalities and psychologies. The effect of this ultra-egalitarianism, this idealistic democracy, was in fact to individualise everything'.

The problems identified by Freeman, Rowbotham and Seyd are not new to the movement. Such difficulties have been recognized by many sections of the socialist and feminist movements over the last 10 years. So why do these problems remain so evidently pertinent? What is the source of this addiction to such a self-defeating mode of (non)organization?

The roots of failure

The determination to reject formal structure in favour of non-hierarchical methods of working has undoubtedly contributed to the collapse of numerous projects in different spheres over the past 10 years. Time, capital and labour have been wasted or lost as groups have burned themselves out.

We wish to understand why these projects failed – at the level of theoretical principle, beyond the circumstances of particular cases. In our view there are two crucial issues:

- One dogma of 'good organization' was replaced by a different dogma. Nobody realized that no dogma is good dogma, and that it's not a question of inventing a new organizational form which is supposed to apply to all situations, but rather of realizing that different situations and tasks require different organizational forms.

- Attention was diverted away from the external product of a collective's efforts and onto the internal process, 'correct' internal politics was taken to 'guarantee' the political effectiveness of the collective's activity.

We can point here to the prevalence of a very dangerous chain of interlinked arguments, or assumptions, along the following lines:

- Capitalism and the so-called socialist states have produced one notion (or dogma) of 'good organization': efficient, hierarchical organization, with a strict division of labour, which is assumed to be good for all situations. Since libertarians wish to model themselves neither on capitalism nor the so-called socialist states, the industrial form of organization with which they are associated is rejected for all situations.

- In reaction, fully democratic, informal, non-hierarchical organization becomes the model for all cases and contexts. Thus we have the replacement of one rigid decontextualized dogma of organization by a different one, with a different *content*, but an equally rigid and decontextualized form.

- Because the end cannot justify the means in the libertarian vision, all the attention is focused on the means. The organizational form, or process, which is supposedly a 'prefigurative form' of the future society being sought, becomes the be-all and the end-all of political concern. And here the central notion is that of the 'collective'. The assumption is that as long as we fight in the right *way* we are bound to win. From here it is only a short step to thinking that it doesn't matter if we win, as long as we've played the game in the right spirit. It is against this perspective for instance, that Neil Kinnock's recent insistence on the priority of the need to gain power shocks many people. There are many questions to ask of Kinnock, but if we continue to be intimidated by the notion of power, to believe that it's more important to keep our hands clean (or at least to 'resign' rather than be implicated in anything less than perfect) than to achieve an imperfect realization of our ideals, we are doomed by definition.

Chapter II

A case-study in failure

Cultural politics in the 70s

So far we have endeavoured to identify the main political currents and perspectives of the 1970s without trying to write a conventional history of the period. We have outlined what we believe went wrong, without giving any clear idea of what we think might have happened if a different set of ideas had prevailed.

In order to do this we will now look at the field of 'alternative' publications. We will look at the economic limitations under which they have either been forced or chosen to work and then take the example of *The Leveller* as a case-study of how the ideas we've been talking about added to the difficulties caused by economic limitations lying outside the control of the magazine. Finally, we look at strategies other publications have subsequently adopted to try to overcome such economic limitations.

A new approach emerged along with the more political versions of the 'alternative' press which grew up in the wake of 1968: a new pattern emerged in which lack of capital was made good by the input of self-exploited labour. Typically, a publication was produced by free labour, which, in combination with donations from supporters in steady jobs, was just enough to get it over its recurring financial crises. The workers were usually volunteers, whose economic needs were low, given their commitment to squatting and 'claiming' as a way of life. This allowed some kind of economic survival at a very low level, but the publications tended to generate no surplus from which the workers' labour might be paid. As a result these publications were either infrequent, badly produced and poorly publicized, or often a combination of all three.

The only other approach seemed to be that of party political publications, where publishing was openly recognized to be an extension of the party's overall work and the problem of finance was seen differently. Subsidy was assumed to be necessary, and self-sufficiency was deemed desirable but unattainable. The 'fighting-fund' approach was (at least until very recently) exemplified by the *Morning Star*'s campaigns, over the last 35 years and Soviet subsidies notwithstanding to keep the paper alive. This approach involves a recognition that, in an advertising-based press system, left-wing political views have to be paid for in another way. A paper like *Newsline* (the daily of the Workers' Revolutionary Party) uses a more disguised form of subsidy (aside from its various cash donations), in that the production workers, whilst paid the union rate for the job, return part of their wages as a donation to the cause.

But any group which wanted to reach a larger audience and did not have the funds a well-organized party membership could generate clearly needed to find another way to raise capital. One of the more worked-out solutions to this problem was the structure of supporting subscribers first used, in recent times, with some success by *The Leveller*.

This involved finding a large number of people who would be willing to part with a small chunk of money to create a larger sum as launch capital for a publication. In exchange, they would, rather like shareholders, vote for a working collective and have a 'democratic' say once a year. This structure – rather like a loose party membership – could also be used to sell copies of the publication.

The main drawback of this approach is the initial cost of raising those funds. It might sound simple to find 1,000 people to give £20, but this actually involves mailing or phoning a group that may well be up to 10 times that size, which 'costs' a substantial amount in labour/resources.

Another major problem for 'alternative' publications was that what they produced was, on the whole, read by a numerically small group of people. For some of these people, producing particular specialist magazines, their principal self-definition has been in terms of gender; for others, race; for others, a particular specialist area of work; for others, sexual preference; for others, locality. Clearly the political work done by these groups, in raising new issues which classical Marxist traditions have signally failed to address, has been of vital importance. However, there remains a further problem which most of these groups have, on the whole, avoided. Despite all their differences, the principal thing which they, and their readers, share is a certain level of educational attainment. In order to consume these products, their readers need an approximately equal level of cultural competence (which it is hard to get outside of the educational system) to that of the producers. The structure of British society being what it is, there is an extremely small number of people with this asset: to this extent the market for these publications is radically circumscribed, and is largely co-extensive with that sub-set of people who, as well as being politically sympathetic, have also passed through the tertiary education sector.

Looked at another way, the economic position of these readers could be seen in commercial terms, as an asset. In terms of achieving viability through the sale of advertising (and it's hard to see any other route to viability, apart from that of even more specialist/up-market/highly priced journals) the relatively privileged economic position of their readers is attractive to advertisers – who are concerned not only with the number, but also with the purchasing power, of the readers they can reach through a given publication. Many of these publications could, in fact, offer targeted advertising to the ABC1 consumers who many specialist advertisers most want to reach. However, this, of course, involves an unwelcome recognition of the limited social base of these publications; a recognition which few, if any, publications in the sector have been willing to make.

There is a further difficulty when considering readerships for 'alternative' publications. When a commercial publisher talks of a specialist publication, it is usually aimed at a whole category of people; say, for the sake of example, gardeners. Now if there are a lot of them and advertisers want access to particular sub-groups of them, that publisher may devise publications aimed at greenhouse gardeners, rose cultivators, or whatever. The point is that once the category has been decided the publisher seeks to launch a magazine that will speak to all those within that category.

By contrast, attempts to publish specialist magazines with a 'political' definition (feminist, socialist, radical or whatever) have concentrated only on talking to those within a given category (teachers, scientists or whoever) whose views more or less coincide with those of the producers. Now if there was a widespread 'radical' culture this would not matter, as presumably those with 'radical' views would be numerous in many different areas.

However, since the starting point is so small, any politically defined specialist magazine will be an even smaller portion of an already tiny market. This can be illustrated by looking at the circulations of the three largest socialist and feminist magazines: *Spare Rib* (20,000), *New Statesman* (23,000) and *New Socialist* (18,000). So, for example, a teachers' magazine for left or feminist teachers (a category you would imagine was numerous) would probably only have a circulation of between 1–2,000 copies; the actual number of readers always being smaller than the total *potential* number of readers. This has two consequences for the revenue generating potential of these publications; they cannot hope to derive much income either from circulation or advertising; for without a substantial circulation, there is no clear advertising base. But, most importantly, they have missed the political opportunity of creating a magazine within which left wing or feminist ideas can operate, but whose readership derives from its competence in satisfying and interesting the whole of its specialist category of readership; in the example we've used, the profession of teachers.

When considering launching a new publication, a capitalist publisher invests first in preliminary market research; a feasibility study; develops a launch plan; and later conducts readership surveys on consumer response in order to shift the publication's 'profile' as necessary. This approach to marketing has largely been rejected by the alternative press; the consequent insulation of publications in this sector from an understanding of who their readers are and how they use the publication has had damaging results.

These are the kinds of elementary propositions about markets, and marketing, which the world of capitalist market research trades in as a matter of course. It could be that the alternative press has much to learn from this discredited world. Without extensive market research how will the feedback between writers and readers ever be improved? Without recognizing what types of people currently read, and don't (or can't) read a given publication, and what aspects of style and presentation of the material people find most difficult, how would it ever be possible to develop more popular editorial policies?

Most of the thinking which has gone on in this sector has come from the perspective of journalists who have been concerned to launch projects in which they were finally able to write the articles they wanted to, free of the restraints imposed by the capitalist owners of publications. It is this same group of people who have been the core of most campaigns around media freedom and opposition to censorship. Unfortunately, this focus on journalistic freedom has meant that all the emphasis has been on the editorial end of the communication process. In rejecting the forms of understanding of audiences and markets which the commercial media work with, these projects have often ended up by completely neglecting the problem of their market. This has meant that they often sustain illusions about the nature of their readership, imagining, for instance, that they communicate with the 'people' or the 'working class' or 'women' in some undifferentiated sense, while remaining wilfully ignorant of the fact that their actual readership is a particular, highly-educated, sub-section of any one of these categories. To think about these problems simply in terms of 'freedom of expression' is, in fact, to take a perspective which derives from debate about artistic freedom. It is one thing to argue that artists should have the freedom of expressing their 'nature', 'souls' or 'egos' in an untrammelled way, but quite another to suggest that journalists should be free to express themselves in this way. What is important is the relationship between writers and readers and the responsibility of the writer to represent the interests (in both senses of the word) of their readers.

Once you think about the problem in this way, then notions of market research and market feedback have a positive use, because they allow you to understand whether you are failing or succeeding in communicating with your intended audience. Commercial market research can certainly be said to produce this kind of feedback in dubious or distorted ways, but without such feedback, a political project insulates itself from the people it is trying to reach. Left and feminist communication projects tend to know very little about their audiences simply because they haven't seen the political importance of understanding their 'market'.

There is a real fear that information derived from readership questionnaires or from more detailed market research is somehow suspect, and that the producers themselves know best. Often they express this by saying they produce the publications for people like themselves.

The political mechanisms that do exist which are intended to generate such 'feedback' – such as readers' meetings, subscriber voting rights, Annual General Meetings, etc. – are held up as a much purer form of dialogue with the readership than that provided by market research. But it is difficult to see how an often self-selecting or random group can be very useful in making adjustments to editorial policy, and few of these mechanisms actually produce real change.

The alternative is surely to convene groups rather like a qualitative market researcher might. So, for example, you might want your magazine to reach women of a particular age or some section of black people. To discover how it would succeed or fail in doing so, you would need to get together a group of actual readers in this category, a group of potential readers from that category, and so on. From the recorded comments of these groups you might decide to make this or that change or attract more readers in the category you've decided to pursue or, alternatively, decide it's unlikely you will be able to attract more of these readers.

But we have to recognize the in-built differences and contradictions of interest between subject of story/writer/editor/publisher/reader – i.e., to recognize these differences and develop mechanisms for dealing with them – treating the resultant conflicts as potentially creative – rather than trying to deny the existence or legitimacy of these contradictions.

The Leveller: collective problems

We now look at how these problems affected one national 'alternative' magazine, *The Leveller*. For our purposes, this magazine was important for two reasons: a) its internal organization reflects the ideas we've been discussing and b) it set out to reach a wider audience than existing, radical publications.

The Leveller started life in March 1975 as a pub discussion between three socialist journalists bemoaning the lack of a good left-wing investigative magazine. The main force behind its launch was Dave Clark, a freelance journalist, whose energy and commitment brought it into being.

In 1975, 10,000 copies of a pilot issue were produced and the launch date was set for Autumn, 1976. Sales started at little over 1,000 and rose to around 2,700 by issue 5. This steady rise in sales was greatly helped by its prosecution with *Peace News* over the naming of 'Colonel B.' during an 'Official Secrets' trial. The publicity surrounding this case took the magazine to its highest point with a print run of 7,000.

Editorially, the magazine created a mixture of politics and culture which has now become commonplace in its successors. Its most distinctive editorial concept was that of 'guerilla journalism'. The idea was that a small magazine would uncover the dirt on somebody and print it because it did not fear the libel laws. Once printed, the mainstream media would get interested in the story and pick it up. In this way, a small magazine could have an impact out of all proportion to its resources. But, in addition, it was interested in cultural politics and in broadening the definition of what was considered political.

The Leveller's innovatory and uneven mixture of ideas produced, among other things, the first set of articles about sex magazines and the fashion industry, a survey of male attitudes to contraception and a detailed look at the rock music industry.

After the 'Colonel B.' trial, the magazine's circulation stayed roughly static, and the meteoric growth of subscription, from just over 100 at its launch to 1,200 two years later – a major source of its operating revenue – began to slow down. This produced the first serious financial crisis for the magazine.

With hindsight, it's possible to draw a connecting line between the magazine seeming to reach the limit of its circulation potential, its recurrent financial crises and the steady demoralization of its original inspiration and talents. This produced a dissatisfaction with the magazine which grew stronger as various of the collective's members began to examine the causes of these difficulties. They began to identify the following problems:

- there was difficulty in producing a magazine to a high standard without a recognition that skills existed and some had more than others

- the inefficiency of the collective process was partly to be blamed on the fact that no person took full responsibility for anything as 'the collective' was theoretically responsible for everything

- that an open collective which anyone could join and participate in (formally) with almost equal weight both slowed down the process of forming a consensus on anything and prevented the group from building up its expertise and skills.

And it was around this last point that the mounting grievances were argued and the collective split in the summer of 1980. In autumn 1980 *The Leveller* decided to go fortnightly, after a long fund-raising campaign which successfully paid off its existing debts (£5,000). The running deficit per issue, which had been approximately £250 per issue in 1977, had risen to £300 per issue by 1981, and because it was fortnightly the new collective had to find £600 each month to keep afloat; something like £8,000 a year all told just to survive, apart from production costs, etc.

In this final phase *The Leveller* added new formal commitments to its politics. As well as capitalism, it was now also against racism and patriarchy. It saw itself as writing about sexual politics in a way which would attract a wider readership of women to its circulation. But these formal commitments did not seem to attract a greater proportion of women readers to the magazine. In its last readership questionnaire the proportion of women to men was still 29%:71%; a proportion remarkably similar to other radical magazines.

The magazine continued to defy financial gravity by running up hefty debts with its suppliers and by obtaining a bank overdraft. Also, the costs of several issues were offset by several large donations. But finally, in the autumn of 1982, it collapsed with debts of £8,000.

Strategy

From the beginning, *The Leveller* was never clear who it was going to be aimed at, or what purpose it served. Discussions of the magazine's politics seemed to waver between lofty discussions of 'the contemporary political situation' and detailed page breakdowns of its contents. So how did it define what it was trying to do?

An early discussion gave an outline.[1]

'The new monthly would concentrate... on the sort of material that does not find its way into the conventional press. We are aware of the whole range of papers from those of the orthodox left... to the community press and rank and file papers and [do] not seek to supersede them. Rather it would supplement them and try to win over new readers to a socialist position.'

This slightly Leninist formulation was later changed to a commitment to reach people outside of the Left, a commitment which was never thought through. The magazine needed to do this because it badly needed the credibility a large circulation would give it in order to get its stories taken seriously. This was tied to the desire to have an influence outside of the left by supplying subversive information to a wider audience. The hippy press, with its quixotic mish-mash of politics, drugs and music also formed an unconscious model. The idea was that people would read, say, the rock music coverage and take in some 'real' politics along the way.

So, without a clear strategy (where the magazine would fit alongside other magazines in the market, who would buy it...) the magazine became a series of constantly competing individual ideas only held together by being within the same magazine.

There was no strategic notion of what it was doing. If you say magazines occupy ideological space, then no-one had defined what space they were trying to occupy or why the magazine's editorial content would be unique enough to do anything like that.

Early on it was decided that *The Leveller* was going to challenge the fundamental premises of the bourgeois press:

'*The Leveller* should not reproduce the forms imposed by the division of labour under capitalism and its reinforcing ideologies. The magazine cannot formulate critiques of the false separation between "the political", "economic", "the industrial" and so on, if it duplicates that typology in its work organization and layout.

We are opposed to rigid sectioning and regular features that *have* to appear in every issue. But there are four general areas in which material can be collected for editing and publication. These are news, agitprop, theory and culture. But we should not fetishise them or present them as separate sections of the paper.'

In practice, this 'cultural revolution' in editorial policy just produced a magazine that looked messy, and slowly 'sections' crept back in. But, because there was no agreement on anything more than the vaguest outline of the balance of articles which should be included, there was neither policy nor ground rules by which to decide whether an article went in.

By seeking to imply that any set of rules was 'bourgeois', the criteria by which articles were selected were reduced to an ad-hoc process. Often an article's merits had then to be argued from first principles, and this was a time-consuming process.

The magazine's uniqueness was defined negatively:

' We are talking about making the whole organization non-capitalist. We are not a commercial publication seeking to profit from a slice of the market and what we are trying to do has not been done before. Making *The Leveller* work will not be easy but we believe the magazine's democratic basis will provide a firm basis for success.'

By consciously excluding discussion of the magazine as a product, the group began unconsciously to paint themselves into an ideological corner and failed to clarify who the intended audience for the magazine was. Underlying this lack of a clear picture of what the magazine was going to be was the problem of distribution:

'To start with, the magazine is going to have to attempt to obtain a "mass" circulation (at least 5,000 or maybe even double that) by selling in the only way that can produce circulation; by selling on news-stands. Here it will compete with capitalism's own commodities which will be far more colourful and alluring for the casual reader; both in price and appearance.'

The most consistent measure of the magazine's ambition was how big it wanted its circulation to be. Some of its original founders talked of a long-term target of 50,000. And there was even talk of printing 25,000 copies of the pilot issue, though this was later reduced to 10,000 copies (and of this 10,000 only three-quarters were ever distributed; many being given away for nothing).

After preliminary investigation, it became clear that no political magazine was selling more than 1,500 copies through the radical/ alternative bookshop network, and also that no serious commercial distributor would touch the magazine. Indeed, because many of the journalists interested in investigative reporting were unwilling to have their stories 'libel-read' even by left lawyers (and saw this kind of thing as a fundamental interference with their individual rights), it was believed that the magazine would never seriously be considered by any of the big three distributors – W. H. Smith, John Menzies and Surridge Dawson.

The alternative was to try and by-pass the existing channels to the marketplace. This the magazine attempted to do by being one of the moving forces in the creation of an organization called Publications Distribution Co-operative. This successfully broadened the radical/ alternative network to the point where it could sell 3–4,000 copies of *The Leveller*, but it failed to make any impact on the mainstream newsagent trade.

The problem for PDC was that it did not have many 'newsagent' magazines, and was unwilling to take on a wider range of magazines to 'bulk-up' its newsagent distribution unless they fitted a rather tight set of political criteria. But it was vital to have a wider range of magazines in order to get taken seriously as a supplier by newsagents. The consequence of this decision was that PDC slowly retreated from this possible area of expansion into the newsagent trade and retrenched, as a supplier to the radical/community bookshop network.

Whatever the political reasons for not approaching commercial distributors, this left the magazine constantly on the fringe of wholesale distribution and so unlikely ever to have a serious chance of getting the wider circulation it needed. Later in its life, when the opportunity to be distributed by W. H. Smith came up, the collective turned it down rather than risk its political integrity for the wider circulation it wanted. W. H. Smith insisted that the copy would have to be checked by lawyers for potentially libellous statements prior to circulation and *The Leveller* collective could not accept what they saw as an infringement of their editorial prerogative.

The Leveller failed to recognize that it would not reach a financial level at which it could survive in the long-term and make an impact on a wider political audience without the distribution channels offered by the major distributors. And when political pressure on these major distributors (through, say, the publication of *Where Is The Other News* and the efforts of the Campaign for Press and Broadcasting Freedom) forced them to accept political publications like *New Socialist* and *Marxism Today*, *The Leveller* failed to follow into the political space opened up.

Looking back, the only alternative would have been to become a largely subscription-based magazine like *New Internationalist*. But this would have required a different set of priorities which would have made marketing a key concern, and would have needed at least £25,000 in launch capital (the sum originally estimated in a founding document).

Finance

Although the magazine's political ambitions were set very high, it never produced a serious budget for what it was going to do or calculated what it might need financially to establish itself. There was only ever a series of over-optimistic projections that no-one used or took seriously. The significance of these seemingly technical matters and the importance of how the magazine's economic base might influence its political ambitions were never really grasped.

There were only a few attempts to discover what a breakeven point for the magazine might be. Breakeven point was not considered important because it was felt that once the magazine was established, its readers (by providing donations) would consider it too politically important to let it die, and would keep it alive by making donations.

The only relatively clear statement of how *The Leveller* was going to fund itself can be found in an early document:

'We are not proposing a community paper financed by a geo-graphically or industrially defined group and neither are we proposing the paper of a political party or tendency. Neither are we arguing for a paper financed by a small group of wealthy liberals...

What is needed is the ability to float the magazine and keep it afloat while it establishes itself. This may take a period of perhaps two or three years, especially bearing in mind the rapid erosion of inflation and the sort of journalism we want to see. Our proposals therefore take the bold and imaginative step of locating the finance and control of the magazine in the hands of its readers.'

By launch date, the magazine had raised £1,680, of which only £160 remained unspent. What strategy there was to overcome this slim financial base can best be described as 'barefoot economics'. This was the idea that because we were engaged in a political project, everything could be done for less money by a voluntaristic effort of will. In this way, we could survive and our hard struggle would ensure us a steady flow of 'moral' capital which later could be turned into real money by fundraising among the broadening base of the magazine's readership.

The other side of the coin of 'barefoot economics' was voluntary labour. Freely donated articles, pictures, cartoons, layout, etc., become one substitute for the lack of capital, and this was supplemented by such capital-saving devices as using a squatted office.

The lack of capital created underdevelopment symptoms that would have an air of familiarity to anybody living in the Third World. Because there was only just enough money to keep afloat with the income from donations and subscriptions, there was never enough money seriously to promote the magazine. So all income went to cover the running costs – so the magazine spent the whole time running to stand still. Any fundraising drive to find capital to expand was swallowed up in the substantial running deficit before it could provide additional funds to finance the expansion. No amount of 'benefits' or appeals to the readers ever produced enough to take the magazine from its hand-to-mouth existence to a higher level of operation.

The real tragedy was that the magazine had two separate points (the legal costs awarded in its favour after the 'Colonel B.' trial and a substantial personal donation) in its life when it was given the sort of funds which would have allowed it to break out of this cycle of underdevelopment. But, because of its attitudes to business and finance, it was unable to seize the opportunities offered.

With a rejection of the capitalist marketplace went a rejection of the importance of business itself. The rotation of the job of Treasurer (everybody's least favourite job) ensured that there was often confusion about the magazine's financial position. To get people to do it, the job was always presented as 'only doing the books and paying the money into the bank'. Few people who did it tried to present an accurate picture of how much the magazine needed to raise over the year, or in which areas it needed to cut costs or increase income.

There was a financial report at every weekly collective meeting, but this was not widely understood, and was often treated as a joke. The main interest in this report was simply to see whether there was enough money for the next issue to come out. Beyond idle dreaming, survival enforced a short-term view. Because the overall position was so desperate, people preferred to avoid the topic of finance, simply because there never seemed to be a solution. It was easier to adopt the happy view of Mr Micawber; something would turn up. Without proper financial reports or any idea of where the magazine's breakeven point was, it was difficult to discuss in anything but the vaguest of political terms whether the magazine was making progress.

Whether the magazine should accept advertising – which later became a major source of revenue – had first to be discussed as a matter of principle, and this debate only started *after* the magazine was launched, which meant that no serious selling of advertising was done for over a year. Many of the early issues had no advertising at all.

A set of problems pursued each others' tails. Without increased circulation, you couldn't find the money to produce better editorial. Without which you couldn't sell more copies, without which you couldn't sell more advertising. To sell more copies, you had to print more copies, which needed money which you didn't have until you sold more copies.

If you want a wider readership, you have to go through the existing channels (with all the attendant compromises) or circumvent them by selling subscriptions direct to your readers, which requires you to make marketing one of the most important priorities. In this context, these kinds of 'commercial' concerns are almost more important than editorial concerns. And a proper concern with business is the tool you use to produce your political ambitions. You cannot produce results just by putting 'politics in command'.

Conclusion

We can generalize from the arguments we've been making. If the aim is to create a different sort of political culture, then publications need to be understood to occupy ideological space. A given political publication should allow a set of political opinions (left, feminist, radical, or whatever) to reach the widest number of people (in the hope of some consequent effect). The most wide-ranging political publication would aspire to be as important as, say, *The Times* or the *Daily Mail*; to occupy some part of the ground occupied by others and, in so doing, deny them some part of their current influence. In the past, the tactic has always been to set up an 'alternative'. These alternatives have included anything from alternative freesheets and alternative listings magazines to alternative TV programmes and so on. But the 'alternative' has usually had a fairly rigid 'political' definition which has circumscribed its potential impact.

We believe that successful political publications should concentrate on attracting and engaging much wider readerships. The price of this may be that the publications launched will have to include and tolerate a far wider range of opinions in order successfully to reach out of the self-imposed 'political' ghettos they have painted themselves into. An example here is the unlikely success of *Marxism Today*. Who would have believed that a journal of the Communist Party with 'Marxism' in its title could sell to double the number of people who are in the Communist Party itself (and without the kind of official distribution which the *Morning Star* finds in the Soviet bloc)? But such a success would pale alongside a publication which could sell to double the number of people who thought of themselves as radical in some way.

The success of *Marxism Today* is based on its ability to engage with (rather than simply ignore or vilify) arguments from a wide political spectrum (including John Alderton, Clive Thornton, Ferdinand Mount,etc.). And if you add to this the way it takes seriously a range of people who fall outside of conventional 'left-right' political labels, you can see how it manages to create a 'public space' for debate where the terms are set from the left. Getting Malcolm Rutherford of *The Financial Times* to review a book about Thatcherism means he is willing to engage in a discussion whose terms he clearly didn't set, but which he nonetheless takes seriously.

And his very participation adds further to the credibility of that framework of debate and the terms within it. It is more important to set the terms and framework of a public discussion than to be seen to win every argument within it. Much of the Thatcher Government's success has been based on understanding this proposition.

There is, of course, a line of objection to all this which says that 'politics' itself is the ultimate determinant of a political publication's success or failure. According to this argument, if a publication accurately reflects the political conjuncture, identifying the key political issues of the day, then its readership will grow. At first sight the argument seems almost common-sensical. Publications clearly reflect the ebbs and flows of political ideas and movements. For example, *Peace News'* decline in circulation, from its heyday in the 1950s, was a clear consequence of the decline of the first post-war peace movement.

But a perspective which is based on identifying the political conjuncture as the key to the success of a publication is ineffective without the economic means to convey any insights derived in this manner. Without this consideration it would be hard to explain why *Peace News'* circulation has failed to grow in recent years in the context of an almost exponential growth in interest in the issues it surveys.

Politically, the most interesting task is the creation of 'coalitions of interest' outside of left, feminist or radical definitions. A good example is the success of *New Internationalist*. Before this magazine started it would have been hard to imagine a constituency of any size interested in issues of development and the Third World. While being a specialist publication, in the sense that it focuses primarily on 'development' issues, from an educational and information point of view, the magazine's editorial policy makes it accessible to the non-specialist reader, and the style of presentation assumes a minimum of pre-knowledge of the area. More interesting still, the 25,000 sales are almost all by subscription (with all the advantages this implies of cash income in advance, and not losing a large percentage of income as discount to the distributor and retailer). This large subscription base has been built up by means of a very positive marketing campaign using direct mail promotions to target sections of the magazine's potential readership.

The examples and ideas presented above are episodic because publishing as an area is not the main concern of this book. But we hope we have shown why the 'alternative' perspectives of the 1970s guaranteed failure and how we might begin to re-examine these problems in the 1980s.

Chapter III

Living in the market

Introduction

Despite fifteen years 'in business' the alternative sector has failed to create a secure economic foundation for its continued existence. This lack of an economic base has been obscured for a variety of reasons. Many ventures survived for some time on the financial backing of wealthy members and supporters – *Ink*, *Red Mole* and *New Left Review*, for example. The majority which did not have such sources of income were able to survive through a combination of loans, political favours in the form of grants from sympathetic bodies and a large-scale input of free labour made possible by low-cost life styles, social security income and squatting.

This could not be a long-term strategy, since such a financial base was vulnerable to both political and economic pressures. The existence of these hidden subsidies obscured the need for radical groups to examine their economic base: they forgot that the economic rug could quite simply be pulled from beneath them. Since they could survive and appear to be autonomous and 'alternative' at a low level of operation, there seemed to be no impetus to change or improve their situation.

With one or two notable exceptions publications and organizations in this sector have almost all been short-lived. They have been based on short-term finance and have given little or no thought to the development of an independent long-term, economic base.* And that is just part of the problem.

Our argument is that we really need to take more responsibility for our own actions and projects. We need to take a harder look at our failures, and to think carefully about how we could, and can, change our tactics by insisting that these areas be fully explored *before* looking for external causes of failure for us to blame. Of course this sector has been bedevilled by its lack of funds, or of access to potential markets, etc., and one must continue to campaign

---

* Significant exceptions to this argument are to be found in the work of organizations such as the Greater London Enterprise Board and the Economic Development Unit of West Midlands County Council, where there has been an attempt to match up socialist/political/ cultural priorities with business skills and investment policies.

to 'change the rules of the game' in favour of the less privileged. But recognizing this should not divert us from also recognizing the need to analyse our own, avoidable, failures and shortcomings, within the limited amount of space that the 'rules of the game' currently make available to us.

Cultural snobbery, commercial ignorance

We believe certain political and economic perspectives have played a major part in locking the radical alternative movement in this country into its own ghetto. Radical movements in France, Germany and Italy have in many respects a better developed infrastructure than their counterparts in Britain.

What is noticeable, particularly in Britain, is the ignorance in the radical movements of how 'the system' works. On the whole, people in these movements know little of commerce, accounting and other business practices. This is partly due to some very crude and irritating forms of cultural snobbery – such as the disdain of commerce and industry among the educated middle-classes. Still prevalent, this cultural rather than political contempt may well be rooted in the landed aristocracy's disdain of the nouveau-riche industrialists of the 19th century.[1]

One might suggest that this cultural snobbery is anti-industrial, rather than anti-capitalist. It certainly takes some quite bizarre forms. For instance, among the 'radical' middle-classes there is often less antipathy to inherited wealth than there is to wealth generated in the present-day market.

Ignorance about the workings of commerce has also been rationalized on the grounds that, if you are doing something politically 'different' – e.g., constructing new organizational forms or developing the 'politics of process' – you do not need to understand the mechanisms of bourgeois business.

These attitudes are clearly at odds with the practical measures necessary if alternative or radical politics are to develop with any commercial success and competence. They are also far from 'radical' in origin, and it is surely unfortunate that their influence in the radical sector should be both so powerful and so unexamined.

Political economy in the ghetto

We would suggest that the key organizational weaknesses of the sector stem from the ideological framework within which most of these organizations were conceived. The political culture from which they emerged had a number of blind spots which made it difficult to conceive of the genuine importance of skills such as financial planning, budgeting, credit control, accountancy, entrepreneurship and management. These skills were seen as 'capitalist' and therefore reactionary by their very nature.

It is sometimes suggested that to take these questions seriously is to 'sell out' to capitalism, as though there was an intrinsic and total incompatibility between learning how to survive and develop in a capitalist market place and remaining committed to an 'alternative' or 'radical' political project. On occasions this has even been translated into an assumption that bad business, or indeed failure, is a sign of political virtue.

Profit, for example, is a problematic concept to many people in the radical movements. It implies capitalism and thus exploitation and is therefore not seen as something for which one should strive. At best the idea of profit is expressed as 'surplus' and remains a pious hope rather than a practical goal. The real aim is 'breaking even'. But these groups fail to realize that in the long run their idea of what constitutes 'breaking even' in fact translates into bankruptcy or increasing self-exploitation, or both. This happens because profit, or surplus, is essential if an enterprise is to be able to acquire or replace capital assets such as cars, typewriters, typesetting equipment, etc. Most capitalist organizations budget for capital costs as a matter of course. Since such items of capital equipment as exist in the alternative sector have usually been acquired with the help of grants, these groups don't have to think about this.

Moreover, by only setting themselves the goal of breaking even, these groups effectively rule out the possibility of expansion from their own resources: of acquiring assets against which to finance expansion. Such a strategy is, however, a prerequisite of financial survival.

Like profits, expansion itself is also a problematic concept. But beyond that, this self-destructive perspective has often meant that organizations have been unable to survive in the first place, let alone to expand their activities to meet their ambitions.

One simple index of this problem is the widely held view of financial accounting as merely an external/legal requirement, with which an organization must comply (in order, for instance, to get its grant renewed) rather than a vital tool for the internal management of the organization itself. Without proper financial planning, cash flows and forward budgeting, an organization has no clear measure against which performance can be judged. One is navigating without a compass – invariably something of a problem. Even if this particular form of compass was invented by capitalists, life without it can be difficult.

The alternative sector displays both a general lack of understanding of capitalism's financial practices and the inability accurately to calculate costs. Everything is improperly costed. Free labour, subsidised premises and grants all disguise real costs – and this is compounded by the feeling that finance is an inconvenient truth, best avoided. This amounts to a plain lack of business sense, disguised by a political rhetoric which attempts to deny these problems are relevant. Creditors are rarely impressed by rhetoric.

To sum up, an organisation's budget can usefully be seen as a numerical statement of its political possibilities. At its crudest, it's no good launching a magazine aimed at half-a-million people if you've only got £1,000 in the bank. Laughable as this example may seem, it's not a million miles away from how many radical groups have actually behaved.

A further set of attitudes are at play here. They are perhaps best described as a cluster of fears and anxieties; the fear of success and the need for failure. Failure is often justified on the basis that you haven't got a chance since the capitalists have it all sewn up. If you fail, it must be their fault. One aspect of such an attitude is that it provides the valuable certainty that there will also be someone else to blame.

Had alternative projects been conceived with the goal of long-term commercial viability, a number of economic calculations would have had to have been made at the outset. Questions of property, investment, building a capital base and developing assets against which to borrow funds for expansion would have been seen as priorities. These questions could have been resolved in tandem with the organization's political ambitions. In fact this did not happen. Rather than taking seriously the economic imperatives deriving from the financial environment within which the organizations functioned, the primary emphasis increasingly moved towards the internal affairs of how the organization operated. Thus, matters of how the operation could be maximally democratic in its internal workings became the dominant and determining consideration. This emphasis also' meant that the range of organizations with whom one could easily work was narrowed down to those who conformed to the 'correct' internal political/organizational criteria.

Too often these organizations have focused exclusively on their internal relations. Instead of developing strategies for winning more space in the popular markets (which would presumably reek too much of commercialism) they have concentrated on building a self-contained 'alternative' world, somehow parallel to and preferably insulated from, the world of commerce. This can only be a recipe for introversion, exclusivity and decay. From this starting point a popular political project, encompassing wider ranges of people, simply cannot be developed. Neither will a movement, speaking only to itself (given that it is numerically small), provide a large enough market to finance the survival of its own institutions. All that lies this way is eternal dependency on various forms of subsidy.

Manager, coordinator or commander?

In a traditional business organization it would be the responsibility of management to develop a strategic overview which could anticipate problems of the kind mentioned above and develop strategies for dealing with them. However, the wholesale rejection of management theory, as part of capitalist ideology, has had the unfortunate effect of throwing the baby out with the bath water. This perspective simply fails to disentangle the role of management as a necessary administrative function within any organization, regardless of its political purposes, from the particular, 'command-structure' form of management which has developed in traditional business organizations. Many collectives have concentrated on sharing out the swabbing of the Titanic's decks but forgotten to post a lookout for the icebergs. The dominant view of management among the radical movements – as merely a command structure capable of passing orders downwards – represents a serious misunderstanding of how management works. The Left avoids the idea of management by calling people 'coordinators' – as if the skill of management was merely that of stopping people bumping into each other.

One crucial function of management in a capitalist enterprise is the clarification of organizational goals and the continuous development and monitoring of strategies to achieve those goals. The problem – of how to clarify objectives, create a strategy to carry them out and find the means to make them happen, is one that few radical organizations recognize explicitly – most just muddle through. The lack of strategic clarity can only be a recipe for disaster, as the history of failure in this sector over the last few years plainly demonstrates.

We believe it is crucial to come to terms with the fact that since we exist in a capitalist marketplace, we must understand how that market works in order to survive and manage within it. Juggling the contradictions between commercial necessity and political ambition may be an uncomfortable experience, but the only other option is either collapse or an existence so marginal as to be irrelevant.

East End Blues

Many of these problems are illustrated in the following account of what happened on the *East End News*. When it was launched in 1980 the *East End News* made bold claims that it would reach a general readership and the team who launched it were able to raise what seemed to be the enormous sum of £23,000 from a wide range of new sources, including the trade unions. Even with this degree of financial support the *East End News* suffered acute problems. A weekly publication cycle demanded getting things right quickly. With weekly production costs amounting to £3,000 – £4,000, the launch capital gave the paper precious little time to establish itself. Mark Lloyd, who sold advertising space on the paper, gives an interesting account of its early days:[2]

'The *East End News* did no extensive market research before launching, or work on identifying a specific target audience within the three London boroughs. More importantly, little attention was given to the paper's commercial infrastructure, such as the need to fully develop and give priority to establishing an effective advertising department to generate the "financial life blood" of the paper. Within weeks not only had the launch capital evaporated but more seriously little new finance had been gained.

On arriving for work in the second week of the paper's life the office was obviously full of people and busy, that is with the exception of the advertising department. All the free labour . . . was involved in the more glamorous tasks such as journalism and photography. The advertising department had to share two telephone lines with everyone else and as for rate cards and vital advertising material, they had simply not been printed in time. In addition, the location of the "department" was a joke, between the telephone switchboard and the reception counter – thus hardly a professional set-up to impress advertisers. For me, the paper failed in the first month due to its inability to capitalise on all the publicity attracted in both the local and national media.'

The lack of preparation had a disastrous impact on the flow of revenue to the paper:

'I found myself in a position where I was selling space, collecting art work, and carrying out the entire administrative work of the department. Not the least of the tasks was the question of invoicing. No plans had been set for who was going to carry out the important task of invoicing the clients. Thus it fell on me to spend over two weeks going over the early advertisers, finding out their addresses, so as to be able to send them a bill! This oversight meant the paper never received 40% of its advertising revenue, since advertisers quickly realised the *East End News* lacked the machinery to pressurise late payers.'

Unable even to chase existing display advertisers, the *East End News* had little hope of attracting classified advertising – one of the staple revenue earners of a local paper. The failure to attend to the need for a commercial infrastructure was also matched in those early days in the area of distribution. It was some weeks after the launch before anyone was interviewed for the job of distribution manager. There were two applicants for the job. One really wanted to be a journalist on the paper and the other was a bewildered youth sent from the Job Centre where the post had been advertised. He had been led to believe the task only involved shifting bundles of paper about and was overwhelmed when its relative complexity was outlined.

Luck and money could have helped to overcome these problems in time, but the paper also faced stiff competition from two other papers; the *Hackney Gazette* and the *East London Advertiser*, each of which had a circulation of over 30,000 per issue.Both were determined to see off this upstart competitor and they deliberately undercut any rates the *East End News* could offer to advertisers. As the *East End News*' circulation slumped from a high point of 14,000 with its first issue to just 4,000 three months later, it had little competitive advantage to offer advertisers.

These problems were compounded by the prevailing attitude to advertising:

'Tower Hamlets Council placed an ad. of coming events in the borough which included a beauty contest. On this occasion the ad. was banned without any consultation with the advertising staff. This action could have been serious since the Council were potentially our biggest customer and, given the manner in which we treated them, could easily have not bothered to return to us . . . If *East End News* had taken the ad. and thus the money but *also* printed an article against beauty contests, then all people within the paper would have been happy. As it was the paper rigidly stood by its interpretation of its principles, rejected the advert and thus lost vital money and alienated an important potential client.'

Profiting autonomously

One of the main long-term objectives of the radical movements, particularly those which grew to prominence from the late 1960s onwards, was the desire for autonomy. Yet many have become highly dependent on grants from central or local government and an odd assortment of quangos and charities. How did this happen? Perhaps because their notion of autonomy was too narrowly defined, based primarily on a concern for personal liberation, which failed to ask where the money to support the project would come from.

The central issue for a movement which aims to be autonomous is how to achieve survival in the capitalist marketplace, without compromising its political objectives. The collective models of working which many groups have developed, out of their concern with prefigurative forms of organization are, on the whole, relatively expensive (in terms of the use of time and resources) compared with the forms of organization used by their commercial competitors. This puts them at a competitive disadvantage in the market.

The question here has to be one of degree (how much collectivity/participation can an organization 'finance' at a given moment and still survive in the marketplace?) The issue cannot be decided by exclusive reference to moral/political absolutes. It is simply impractical to take the position that such-and-such

'is a politically regressive mode of organization and must be avoided at all costs, and that collective democracy is politically correct and therefore must be adopted regardless of cost.'

Not all moves away from hierarchical forms of organization with a strict division of labour are *necessarily* less cost-effective – witness the reorganization of the labour force into work groups, etc., in various big car-making plants in Europe during the 70s. The point is simply that one needs to be clear about the economic consequences of the political decisions that are made at any point (unless you have a magic wand that will enable you to defy financial gravity).

Movements in the alternative sector share many of the dilemmas of Third World countries. Deciding on a political strategy is only the beginning – the problem is how to finance such strategies: how to avoid relations of dependence on external finance which will jeopardise autonomy; how to juggle contradictions so as to create an inch or two of space in which to operate autonomously; how to ensure your long-term autonomy, survival and development. This is not simply an argument in favour of pragmatism and against idealism, but rather an argument against a form of moralism rampant in this sector – a moralism which has had the over-weening arrogance to identify itself as the 'One True Way to Salvation' and to damn all others who veer from that path.

We make this point forcefully because, on the whole, this sector has failed to pay anything like enough attention to developing its economic base. Indeed, the argument goes further – these kinds of questions have usually been relegated to the bottom of the agenda, or indeed excluded from the agenda of political discussion within the sector – as merely 'mechanical' or technical problems, to be dealt with, if there's time, after the 'policy' meeting, and otherwise left 'till the next meeting'. All too often the creditors have arrived before that meeting.

Just because capitalists are concerned with efficiency and cost-effectiveness it doesn't mean that we have to abandon these concerns in favour of good old-fashioned socialist inefficiency. We need to rescue what is valuable here: we may be motivated by a desire to develop efficient mechanisms to sell a lot of papers in order to make a lot of political impact, rather than to make a lot of money. Either way, resources being scarce, we need to be cost-effective. Of course, that raises a set of difficult questions about the criteria to be used to assess efficiency; of how to distinguish the display of 'efficient action' from what is often less spectacular but more cost-effective; but these are the issues to which we urgently need to address ourselves.

More than that, even, we surely need to generate a surplus, over and above our immediate needs; to generate what, under capitalism, is called 'profits'. We need to make profits for three reasons: to provide some part of the social wage, benefits, etc.; to provide self-generated capital for expansion; to provide collateral for borrowing, either directly from domestic financial institutions or, in a national context, to provide the relevant credentials to international financial institutions and banks. We need to generate profit or surplus, not least, to secure our political independence from the state. Any movement of 'independent' cultural workers which is dependent on state funding is in a precarious position. But that is the corner which large parts of the radical movements of the 70s have backed themselves into.

Chapter IV

The collective decides ...

Introduction

For ten years the political rectitude of a collective method of working has been largely unquestioned. Nevertheless, a number of problems and issues have emerged in this method of working. We offer here a schematic account of these problems as we have encountered them in our own experience. Our emphasis is deliberately negative. We do not wish to decry the concern with democratic and accountable structures of organization which gave rise to collectives, but we feel that many of the problems have gone unstated for far too long. We are glad to add our contribution to the 'rethinking' process which is now starting to happen.

The libertarian obsession with 'process politics' leads to an obsession with all aspects of internal structure and its working. As a result, the collective can often lose sight of its larger political objectives and stress the primacy of the form of organization over the political objectives it was set up to meet. This often occurs in two stages. At the outset the collective process is regarded as equally important to whatever political purposes the group might have. Later the process itself often comes to be seen as of primary importance in a way which is perhaps best understood as an over-reaction to the subordination of the individual to the outward political aim which characterises traditional party political structures.

Even though many people in such collectives will readily admit that the process is inefficient and messy, it is nevertheless often held to be more 'democratic'. From this position it is a short step to claiming that the process is morally superior to the 'bourgeois' way of doing things and therefore cannot be called into question. At this point the group finds itself trapped. A discussion of doing things differently, within the realms of the 'morally acceptable', is no longer possible.

We believe such a discussion to be vital. Specifically, we believe that unless some of the recurring problems of collective working are recognized and resolved, the entire sector may soon be a matter of historical interest only.

Two distinct forms of collective, the 'open' and the 'closed', have emerged, each regarded by their respective supporters as the only proper way of doing things in the debate over community projects.

Those in favour of open collectives argue that unless you give the widest possible range of people open access to the collective you will exclude some category or constituency who deserve representation. Any discussion of restriction of access to the production process is seen as a betrayal of faith in what is held to be the purest form of democratic politics. By contrast, a closed collective is seen as elitist and self-perpetuating.

The open collective has, however, several problems. In an open collective you are continually caught between the need to explain things to the newest member and to help them integrate into the group's work and the need to get on with the task in hand. As the Newsreel Collective put it:[1]

'We have never had the time, nor money, to retrain one another thoroughly in the skills we don't possess, let alone to provide one another with the opportunity of "wasting" film by allowing ourselves to make a lot of mistakes in gaining experience. In any live shooting situation, especially one that cannot be repeated, it's a horrible choice to have to make – between someone who needs to learn how to use a camera but might fuck it up, and someone who already knows and is more likely to get what we need on film.'

The open collective's emphasis on integration and involvement of every member usually means that you can never go faster than the pace of the newest or slowest person in the group.

Further strain is placed on the system by the fact that members of such collectives are often volunteers. Few people have the necessary time to devote to the task in hand, so large parts of the effective work of the collective will tend to devolve on to a small, highly committed group. The same kind of structural conflict of interest emerges in many projects between the paid workers and their management committee. This is also the underlying issue in many of the debates over whether to constitute a collective as a workers' coop or a member/users' group.

Such conflict frequently results in tension between those who know they will be doing the work and those who are there only for the generalized discussions of overall policy; between those who do most of the practical work and feel they have a better view of what is happening, and those who want political influence but are unable or unwilling to give a lot of time to the group's practical work.

The result is often that the most important practical decisions are taken outside the formal group meeting and ratified at a later meeting. The formal group meeting thus functions merely as a rubber stamp – it adds a 'democratic' seal of approval to *de facto* decisions that have already been made. Things often develop to a point where the group's work process itself becomes one long plenary session where everything is open to discussion and decision at every point, rather as if the House of Commons were to try to run an airline by debate.

A further problem is the frequent lack of clear discussion over policy options: often the very notion of being clear about what your policy objectives are is tainted with all the evil connotations of machismo and 'power'. A polarized discussion will be presented in such a way as to blur differences. Moreover, this whole process (especially when merged in a 'consensus' decision-making procedure which excludes the possibility of decision by majority vote) encourages people to say similar sounding things when they actually mean the very opposite. Equally bad, it often leads to a use of language that serves to obscure sharp differences of opinion so that at least the work at hand can carry on.

Worse still, however, the failure to present clear policy options often means that a collective will try to 'contain' two or more entirely conflicting factions, none of which can be given permission to implement what they believe in. The 'no-vote' principle implicit in the commitment to consensus decision-making also allows a vocal minority to give the impression of commanding greater support than they actually do, and allows such a minority to prolong the discussion beyond the point at which they would have any hope of gaining a majority for their views.

Without a forum in which formal policy of any kind can be made, there will usually be, by default, a kind of *de facto* policy-making by a network of personal friendships which is able to utilize the confusion built into the process. The only formal record of the decision-making process is often the minutes of the collective meeting. Since these won't necessarily represent the necessary day-to-day decisions taken during the group's actual work, there can often be immense confusion over what decisions have been taken.

If a collective meeting is too obviously divided, a problematic issue will often be deferred to give the collective more time to reach a consensus. Such a process does not allow decisions to be taken quickly on controversial issues. This poses no problems in a self-contained discussion group, but if the collective in question is trying to produce a service or product for the outside world – a café, a cinema, a magazine – it can cause obvious difficulty. Quite simply, the outside world will not necessarily take heed of Canute-style gestures indicating that the collective needs time to arrive at a consensus. The democratic impetus behind the notion of collectively discussing and deciding things is certainly important, but in order to survive, an organization must be capable of taking key policy decisions quickly when the situation demands it. Too often the commitment to 'consensus' pre-empts that possibility. Different situations demand and allow different decision-making procedures, and the 'principled' adherence to one (collective/consensus) method in *all* situations is a recipe for disaster.

Often the formal lines of responsibility in radical projects/groups bear no resemblance to where or how decisions are actually taken. This is an inevitable consequence of setting up 'ideal' structures that don't correspond with the reality of the needs of the group's practical work. To the outsider who wishes to join the collective the situation can be even more confusing. You won't be dealing with one person; everyone may be willing to talk to you, but few will take individual responsibility for a decision: chiefly because the very notion of individual responsibility is usually ruled 'out of order' by the collective ideology. This lack of clearly defined responsibility is a frequent cause of rancour – it means that it's very hard to trace the source of a mistake since nobody can be found to accept individual responsibility. Everyone produces either pragmatism or default as reasons why a particular thing didn't happen.

The lack of individual responsibility is related to another unwritten article of the libertarian constitution: the desire to rotate all jobs in order to prevent individuals building up power. Power, rather than the way in which it is exercised, is often seen as a thing in itself. As a result, people will only take responsibility on a partial basis.

The voluntary nature of a collective can also result in a particular task often being forced on someone or given to an unknown newcomer. It is then difficult to demand that this person takes full responsibility for that task. More importantly, because the jobs are often constantly taking part in a kind of 'pass the parcel' rotation, they are never seriously defined, because such a definition would imply the kind of sole responsibility which is anathema to a collective that wants everyone to feel equally responsible for everything. But without clear job definitions it is impossible to call to task somebody who isn't doing their job. Everything is equal and shared, but no one is directly accountable for anything.

There is a worrying definition of 'equality' implied here. In this context the struggle to establish equality takes on a new dimension as, in effect, the struggle to abolish all differences. The starting point seems to be the notion that different degrees of power are to be abhorred. As the individual possession of knowledge and skills is a source of power in any organization there is often an attempt to eradicate all differences of knowledge or skill within the group. But as the possession of knowledge or skill is something which people are made to feel guilty about, they often can't admit that they have them, which, among other things, makes it difficult for them to share their skills with others. The fact that commitment to collective solidarity is a key value tends to increase the pressure for people to adopt the same views or, at least, to repress their differences. This makes constructive debate difficult within the group, and leads easily to a situation in which the repressed differences finally explode and the collective splits in an ironic parallel of sectarian organizations to which the collective was seen as an alternative. In short, what we have here, and we cannot prevent the Kampuchean overtones, is 'equality' re-modelled as the suppression of all difference.

Accountability and the rationality of bureaucracy

At the heart of the matter is the problem of defining responsibilities in radical projects. The present pattern is one in which undefined responsibility is too lightly undertaken without considering the nature of the job and whether, for example, a volunteer is the right person to do it. And when things start going wrong it becomes even more difficult to reallocate responsibility.

Experience shows that clear patterns of accountability are crucial if a collective is to function effectively. So if, for example, the task is to sell advertising space and after an agreed period the individual responsible has not sold any advertising space, he or she should be asked to account for their failure to do the job effectively. Then we need to discover whether the problem arose because the job was delegated to the wrong person, or whether it was because the job itself was badly defined, or whether there are external factors which mean that the job cannot be done by anyone until the circumstances have changed.

But accountability means more than simply apportioning blame to certain individuals. It also means developing an organizational culture which will encourage the individual in question to be the first to bring the problems to the attention of the collective. This requires a working atmosphere in which the admission of personal inadequacy or failure is not necessarily regarded as culpable.

At this point we could also refer to Max Weber's arguments for the *rationality* of bureaucratic procedures – in so far as they usefully distinguish, for instance, between the role and the particular person filling that role at a given moment.

One of the strengths of a bureaucracy is that it will develop explicit rules and procedures, written down in rule books, which can be shown to newcomers to the organization, who can thus take over a new function without too much trouble. Our argument is that in relation to 'bureaucracy' (and in relation to the division of labour) the left has, on the whole, only got *half* of the argument. Bureaucracy may have depressing aspects and ironically the left shares some of these, but it also has some vital points on its side. For instance, it is quite normal for a crisis to occur when a worker leaves a community project. No one else can effectively take over from them, because all the information, contacts and criteria of decision-making are inside their heads, rather than explicitly formulated in a way that makes them accessible to others. You have to start with the premise that since no one is irreplaceable, other people will be able to understand what is in his or her head, and to establish a system for making that knowledge generally available. If you don't start on that basis it will be too late when you realize why you should have done. Or, as someone said, an organization that does not secure the conditions of its own reproduction is doomed within a generation.

Voluntary disorganization

Many collective or cooperative organizations in the voluntary sector were formed in the social welfare or community development field in the seventies and were also influenced by the political, libertarian culture of that period. However, it is noticeable that the style of collectivity operated by many of the voluntary organizations frequently resembles more closely that of professional partnerships or companies, rather than the earlier experiments in workers' control with which they often identify themselves.

The style of self-management practised in much of the voluntary sector is in many respects quite different to that of the collectives discussed earlier: it reflects the highly-educated and self-confident background of the people involved in these organizations – people who are not about to be told what to do by anyone else if they can avoid it. In some such organizations this difference becomes institutionalized: membership of the collective group, for example, might be limited to the professional workers, while other functions, such as clerical and secretarial work, are contracted and managed on a conventional hierarchical basis.

Damaging collisions can occur between supporters of this style of self-management in social or community work, and the very people they are working to help. This was illustrated by a letter in the *Hackney Gazette* in January, 1984. It was written by an outraged member of the local community, who complained that the local community centre was closed for the whole of the Christmas week. Here, as the embittered author put it, was a bunch of educated, middle-class lefties organizing their cooperative working rules to suit what the author perceived as simple self-interest. Everyone else in the area either had to work or to suffer unemployment during the Christmas period, yet the centre was run by a group of people who were able to make the rules to suit themselves – a self-indulgence they justified on political grounds. While we pass no judgement on the fairness of this complaint, the form in which it was expressed – conflict between traditional working-class expectation and middle-class self-management – is certainly worth noticing.

This conflict has other manifestations. Many of these organizations have offices which are ablaze with posters and lapel badges asserting a progressive and radical politics. This sort of display defines and expresses the politics of the organizing group, but it seems possible, at the very least, that it will also work to intimidate many other people who, while far from rabidly Tory, do not exactly share these explicitly asserted faiths, and this can work against any possibility of developing the involvement of a wider public, or of expanding the constituency of the political ideas one supports. In some respects, the recent increase in the number of paid community work posts in many inner city areas, which is also a consolidation of the political culture we are talking about, may actually be working to increase the distance it was intended to close. Harmonious relations between the managers and the managed in voluntary sector organizations may have been possible during the community development drive of the early seventies. They have certainly faltered, with the hardening political and economic climate of the eighties, and we have recently seen a return to a more militant trade unionism within the sector. In some depressing cases, ex-community workers have even ended up taking management committees (which they themselves had struggled to form a few years earlier) to industrial tribunals, in disputes about their own personal terms and conditions of employment. The mobilization of the heavy machinery of industrial relations against management committees can be perverse if it results in a less educated, less politically adept group of voluntary people (*not* always representatives of the local state) being crudely thrust into the role of 'management'. A similar failure of political integrity may well be involved in the recent blocking by local government officers of attempts to decentralize Labour controlled administrations through 'going local' initiatives, involving area offices. As a recent and welcome pamphlet from the Labour Coordinating Committee puts it:[2]

'When cuts and privatisation are on the top of the agenda, if you're not going to work in a way that is appropriate to the needs of the community you serve, they will have no reason to support you when your job is on the line.'

(Labour Co-ordinating Committee, Go Local to Survive: decentralisation in local government, *p. 25)*

Political guarantees

The alternative/libertarian sector has been dominated by an extremely slipshod approach, often involving a lack of attention to the specific skills of the task in hand. Sometimes this results from the assumption that a person's 'correct' political views will guarantee that they can do any given task. This is, of course, a most unhelpful form of moralism, which derives from a generalization of concerns such as politics and morality, which may well be the proper priorities in some contexts, to a perspective in which they function as the determining priorities in all situations. The need to distinguish between the person and the particular task is often bypassed. This distinction has often been blurred by the libertarian version of the argument that the personal is political. The person in question may have an impeccable political stance on racism, sexism, etc., and still be lousy at packing parcels or writing reviews, or whatever. The converse is, of course, also true. It may be that a group wants to insist that a person should be good at doing a task *and* possess a particular set of political views, or inhabit a particular lifestyle. But that then has to be seen as a *supplementary* or *additional*, not an *alternative* qualification. The priorities chosen here have to be chosen consciously, and their likely effects fully understood.

The personal is surely political (how could it not be?), but the political extends some distance beyond the personal (into the 'public'); nor is the personal capable of simply being reduced to the political. One consequence of the dominant libertarian perspective here (as you are 'living a project', not 'doing a job') is that you can't criticize anyone's performance of a particular task without it being seen as a total attack on the person. It thus becomes impossible to distinguish 'doing a bad job' from 'being a bad person'.

From this perspective 'politics' becomes a guarantee of ability or, conversely, proof of inability. The bones of libertarian Stalinism perhaps, with a different content, and different views being prescribed, but a similar form, where there is only one road to salvation and all other roads are seen to lead to the libertarian equivalent of Hell.

The collective attitude to skills

'Another pitfall we've come across is the argument that, because bourgeois theatre is skilful, the development of skills is bourgeois. It is even sometimes argued that a lack of skill is good because it de-mystifies the theatrical process. When we first started, there was a low level of skill in the group ... for quite a long time we rationalised this stage of development (which most groups go through) into a historical dogma. Eventually, we realised that the belief that if your ideas are correct then it "doesn't matter" how well or badly you put them over, is false ...

This belief that skills ... (are) irrelevant is rooted in the argument that as *socialist* theatre workers we merely *happen* to use theatre to communicate political objectives. This disrespect for the forms used does a disservice to the ideas being communicated. No craftsman would disregard the tools of his trade to the extent that socialist theatre workers often disregard theirs.'

Richard Seyd – 'The Theatre of Red Ladder',
*(*New Edinburgh Review, *August 1975)*

The collective attitude to skills is often derived from the notion that you can create an island of prefigurative, libertarian socialism in a sea of bourgeois practices. The logic of this idea is that the group tries to do everything itself, attempting to control as many parts of the production process as it can manage. This is partly pragmatic in origin. For example, in a publishing project it seems cheaper to sit at the typesetter yourself if your labour is voluntary, even if this does produce very error-ridden copy requiring considerable time and effort to proof-read and correct. But this pragmatism is often elevated into a point of political principle. It is a short step from there to thinking it is morally/politically correct to do everything yourself – an attitude which blurs into one where there is a marked reluctance to 'put work out' because it somehow implies 'losing control'. It might, in fact, be much more cost-effective to put certain tasks out to firms providing specialist services but this is often ruled out (over and above the cost argument) for 'moral' reasons. Enormous time and resources are then diverted from resolving central policy issues, simply because the collective has failed to find a way of getting the immediate tasks done efficiently.

Are skills a good thing?

Behind the attitude that good politics will produce good works lies a particular attitude to skills. Everybody, with help and mutual criticism, is seen as capable of becoming competent at any task. The work process in the voluntary collective begins to resemble one long night-school class. Some graduate, others don't, and the exam results are often painfully clear in the results of the group's work, as it becomes impossible for a group to accumulate enough skills to take it beyond a certain minimum level of activity.

Weekend schools are often suggested as a 'solution' to the uneven spread of skills. While they can be useful forums in which to discuss problems, they are a quite inadequate means of solving the underlying difficulties which such collectives often face.

Skill-sharing and learning in such a context can only be given a very small amount of time and resources compared to the length of formal courses necessary to teach these skills, or to the substantial budgets available in commercial companies for in-service training. In fact, the 'weekend school' approach often merely emphasizes the gap between the 'quick performers' who learn fast, and the rest who never acquire what they came for.

Another difficulty here which has not had much of a public airing derives quite simply from the fact that the people in a collective will tend to be starting from different and often unequal positions. Quite simply, as a result of all the factors that have structured the collective members' lives prior to entering the group, some will have more skills/knowledge than others. The catch is that it's far easier to move directors to take their turn making the tea, and quite another expecting the typists to take their turn doing the cash-flow projections.

How to share the skills you can't admit to having

Skill-sharing is often made more difficult simply because no-one can admit to having skills or knowing more than somebody else without putting themselves in an unfavourable and ideologically 'illegitimate' power relation over that person. The Newsreel experience is informative here as well:[3]

'The other problem is in how to democratise what used to be "directorial" skills – skills in conceptualising and ordering the material. In theory we wanted to assume that these skills were possessed by everybody – this goes to the heart of our politics. Those of us who had previous directing experience tended to negate our skills, or abdicate – at the same time as in fact possessing a lot of power in practice at grasping how the material might be structured.

In fact, for a long time we hardly ever admitted as a collective that these skills even existed, especially when they had only existed in such an alien world as the film industry. The result was that people *without* these skills or experiences were assuming responsibility for films and were finding them an immense and crushing burden because it was more than they could cope with...

We had been tending to deny differences in skill and experience, and that was leaving us with no basis for learning from one another. The people with the experience were crippling themselves because they felt ashamed of it, and the people without that particular experience were feeling like they were *individual* failures because they couldn't cope... Now we would think it more important to acknowledge differences of skills and experience so as at least to open up the possibility of teaching, rather than to assume away the differences. (This means, incidentally, that we don't think that just "anyone" can be a film-maker; anyone can be a film-maker, but it can take time. This has made it harder for people to join us as a group without previous film experience)... "Collectivity" can become a moral stick with which to suppress difference.'

If a group wants to get involved in skill-sharing, there's a need to acknowledge that some people do have more skills and knowledge in particular areas and to realize the need for proper training. Once you have a 'bourgeois' skill you can decide what you do with it. Many libertarian groups seem to have been unable to make up their minds whether or not the skills themselves were irredeemably tainted.

The dominant assumptions seem to have been that since capitalism produced the division of labour, then that is an exclusively capitalist method of working and not to be touched by an alternative form of organization. Some argument is needed to re-establish the premise that there are, in fact, real and valuable skills which people need to learn, over time, and that the development of specialized skills is not intrinsically bad. Moreover, anyone who wants to abandon the benefits of specialization needs to be very aware of just how much they're losing. These skills, and the professional structures within which they exist, may have bad associations, but that doesn't mean that they can be abandoned without enormous costs.

The libertarian left has often seemed to think that it could solve all problems of inequalities caused by the division of labour and inequality of skills by simply declaring the problem null and void. Rotate all skills. Keep everyone moving so that power never aggregates. One of the Maoist sayings from the Cultural Revolution touched a chord: 'Send the professors into the fields.'

The net result of this was to give the idea that all skills were a clever bourgeois con. No training was needed. It meant that every voice was equal, even in discussions where one person knew the answer and no-one else knew anything about the area under discussion. While this pathologically *ultra*-collectivism may indeed be less prevalent now than 10 years ago, we know for sure that in 1984 it was still possible for a member of a resourcing agency to be invited to attend a meeting of community organisations, only to find the meeting deciding – for reasons of 'equality' – that somebody altogether different should be detailed to phone that very same resourcing agency after the meeting to see what they had to offer . . .

In short, this perspective represents the ultimate logical extension of the environmentalist pole in the nature/nurture debate: people are assumed to have *no* talents, predispositions or specific experience, and to be infinitely malleable – all that is needed is the right environment and the right collective procedures. This is Year Zero, the year of Robespierre and Pol Pot, in which life is to be remade anew, and all trace of past inequalities expunged through collective labour. But at what cost?

Chapter V

Looking at management with a jaundiced eye

Life gets pretty bad down in the collective, but isn't the very idea of management altogether worse?

We believe that an adequate theory and practice of organizational management is vital to the development of a radical political culture in Britain. We also believe that the left has only the most negative ideas in this area. Management is conceived variously as what the enemy does: as a set of techniques which are used to stabilize hierarchical regimes; as a form of rationalization ; or as intelligence which should belong within the labour process but which, in its managerial form, is wielded from above as a controlling set of constraints on the debased and 'de-skilled' activities of modern work. Management is identified with autocratic authority and then dismissed out of hand: it is hardly ever considered as the *relative* authority which is necessary if any differentiated activity is to be carried out. And while the instinctive dismissal of everything to do with management goes on, very little thought has been given to the question of how we might better run our own small organizations and projects or, for that matter, how a better regime of management in large productive or bureaucratic organizations might actually work. We have some thoughts on these matters but, to begin with, it seems worth asking what exactly the current ideas on management are. What is orthodox management theory and where does it exist? And is there anything to be learned from this distant and disapproved source, or do all who drink from this well get instantly poisoned? Let us start by looking at what is taken to be good management in commercial and public sector organizations.

There is certainly a body of thinking about organizational management – one which can draw on a tradition of research and theorization (of sorts) which goes back to the beginning of the century. Despite its occasional attempts to dignify itself as 'theory', however, the important management thinking is fiercely pragmatic. This pragmatism is not just a reflection of its concern to be an applied knowledge; nor is it only the result of a conscious or formulated refusal to ask any really fundamental questions of the organizations it would address. The point is that while there may well be a few critical or independent academic researchers working away here and there, and while there is also a solid tradition of industrial sociology, the really effective and influential management thinking will be found elsewhere – among people who – whether they are independent management consultants or business school faculty members – very often make their living directly from organizations about which they may also write an occasional paper now and then.[1]

This is not simply a world of applied theory at the level of its subject matter; it also involves often enormously lucrative consultancy and training activities which need a touch of theory for their own development and legitimation. This imposes limitations of two types. First, the successful 'management' theory will be the one that is acceptable to the organizations which pay the bill. The fact that as many cranks as sharks swim through the murky waters of management training and consultancy reflects this limitation. In a situation where the real terms of organizational life (and here we mean the political terms) are necessarily not raised into view, is it surprising that a search for 'truth' and 'authenticity' should take place, even if it is displaced into all sorts of semi-therapeutic and psychological vocabularies?

The second type of limitation which derives from this close connection between management thinking and the well paying object of its rumination has to do with communicability – with what can be sold in a 'consultancy' or 'training' package. 'Theoretical' innovations very often bear the stamp of this context. They are likely to be presented in the form of 'logos' and pseudo-theoretical models which can form the basis for two- or three-day training courses. Thus, in amongst all the behaviourist and humanist rhetoric ('management by objectives', 'job enrichment', etc.) this weird world is full of patented or copyrighted 'managerial grid' systems (Concern for People graphed against Concern for Product), Venn diagrams and other such paraphernalia. Even such old hand-me-downs (the classics of this pragmatic 'theory') as Maslow's *Hierarchy of Needs*, McGregor's *Theory X and Theory Y* (people need whipping versus people are better at whipping themselves) or Herzberg on motivation and 'hygiene factors', find a place here – squeezed neatly onto a single sheet of paper or a slide for overhead projection.

One of the main functions of this management theory is to legitimize structures of power and authority which would probably be contested if presented directly. For this reason, management theory needs to be communicable in a slightly different sense as well. It needs to be broadly acceptable to a wider group of people than simply top management – it needs, in other words, to be acceptable to both managed and managers. It is in this far from academic connection that a broad consensus on organizational management seems to have been forged over the last 20 or so years. We are not suggesting that there is formulated agreement on particular issues in this area, but rather that a broadly accepted model and set of assumptions about organizational structure and technique have emerged – almost a commonsense understanding of what management is or should be, of what it is to be organized.

If one assumes the perspectives of this understanding, then there certainly won't be any questioning of the basic terms on which organizations are conducted or, more specifically, of the political disposition in which they exist (perhaps this is why 'analysis' in this world is firmly equated with 'paralysis'). These questions are simply bracketed out – acknowledged, if at all, in asides – or obliquely in dealing with externally determined matters like the contract of employment and its regulation by law. But if politics – not just that increasingly problematic 'expropriation of surplus value', but a wide range of questions relating to organizational regime – are not acknowledged, it also seems important to recognize a certain complexity in this denial. For if political issues are certainly denied, it is significant that they are also not asserted by 'managers' in any hard or driving way. There is little blatant celebration of power in this management thinking, although of course there are exceptions to this. In Britain there is the Aims of Industry/Institute of Directors axis, the Michael Edwardes school of management (which starts, at least at British Leyland, by kicking the consultants *out* and which talks of lean, trim and disciplined workforces), and a number of designedly coercive management consultancies (we have recently come across the semi-literate newsletter of 'Irenicon', a Mayfair-based consultancy firm which runs courses in a series called 'Management's Right to Manage on Discipline and Control', and which includes among its range of services the dispensation of advice on ways of sacking genuinely sick employees). Wide as the range of exceptions may be (and in Thatcher's years it has widened considerably), however, it seems that the more consensual position remains far from explicitly coercive in its understanding.[2] It may be riddled with carefully-maintained blind spots but, to the extent that these blind spots leave it able to think at all, it still prefers the idea of carrots (even extremely tired ones) over sticks. It will argue that carrots are more 'efficient' than sticks, to use one keyword from this world.

Soldiers and sailors: leaders and led

A view of management which is representative of this mainstream in Britain is the one which is credited to John Adair, a man who emerged into the world of management from Sandhurst, where he had been a lecturer in the years after the Second World War. Like many management thinkers, Adair uses military organization as a model for civilian business and administration (he is also a 'historian' of sorts, having written books on military history). Contrary to what might be expected, the reason why Adair is inspired by the military model is not because he sees it as a form of organization in which a coercive efficiency and naked command structures are possible. This may well be part of the truth, but his more important claim is that you can't have a good and effective army – or even a tight ship – without good lines of communication following the line management structure (downward *and* upward in this non-unionized world), effective leadership (instead of the bare exercise of power) and the participation of small, motivated 'teams'. It is all a matter of winning the hearts and minds of (and the word is still automatic) men. From Sandhurst, Adair moved to the Industrial Society, an ostensibly bipartisan industrial relations training organization. There he developed 'Action-Centred Leadership' – a training course which is aimed to make leadership skills available to industrial and public sector managers or supervisors, and which has gone on to turn over millions of pounds.

Action-Centred Leadership was aimed to take the attributes of charismatic (and mostly military) leadership and present them in a more civil version as acquirable 'skills' or 'functions'. 'Communication' replaces power. 'Leadership' stands in for more autocratic styles of management. The point is to see people as a resource, and to get results *through* them. Motivation, therefore, becomes a major issue. It is in this connection that we see the return of heroic figures from the imperial past.

Their stories usually come into the account in a highly mythologized form. Adair draws on historically significant leaders like Churchill, Field Marshal Lord Slim, RSM John Lord (British 'leader' of Stalag XI B prison camp in World War Two), Montgomery, Attlee, T. E. Lawrence, Hunt of Everest.[3] And even if the 'functions' which Adair draws from these stories are ordinary and prosaic (it is precisely of their essence to be straightforward and accessible), the stories themselves are full of personal and national allure and romance. Even the most boring and routinized experience of supervision is full of imaginative possibilities. Together with team games involving Lego bricks and jigsaw puzzles, the Action-Centred Leadership course also uses the war film *Twelve O'clock High*, so that even the lowest grade of industrial supervisor can go to work dreaming of the US Airforce and Flying Fortresses. It is, doubtless, also significant that at the time when Adair's course was first developed, many workers ('men' indeed) had direct experience of national service, if not memories of military life at war – useful grist to the mill.[4]

What exactly are the leadership 'functions' which Action-Centred Leadership seeks to propagate? The question leads us to the Adair/Industrial Society mantra. Printed on a million plastic flashcards designed for supervisory pockets and wallets, this consists of a series of three interlocking circles which can be mapped out as follows:

The argument is that the effective leader secures and maintains an equilibrium between these three circles – ensuring that they are in balanced relationship, and that no one circle becomes too dominant, or falls out of view. The theory behind this is , of course, simple enough. People (or rather 'men') have 'needs' in these three areas. They have individual needs for satisfaction, stability (in and outside the work place), perhaps even 'personal' development, and for skills relating to their work. Similarly, people need to be aware of themselves as active and integrated members of a 'team'. This, of course, is not a recognition of collective interests in any trade union sense – the idea instead is that management should provide a sense of solidarity, purpose and integration *within* the humanized structures of authority and power – a solidarity which may indeed thrive on competitiveness and shaming strategies within the 'team'.

Finally, people need to know what they are aiming to do (their objectives) and also to be able to identify with and receive recognition for their work. This applies to both managers and managed. Work, once the overall objectives are clear, is to be defined in terms of particular 'tasks' which can be clearly identified, measured and regulated on an individual basis. Similarly, rewards and incentives remain individualized.

A more detailed list of the leadership 'functions' within each of the three circles is provided by Edwin P. Smith in his description of Adair's Action-Centred Leadership course:[5]

(a) *Achieving the Task*

The efficient leader,

* is clear what his task is and understands how it fits into the long-term and short-term objectives of the organization.

* plans how to accomplish it,

* defines and provides the resources needed,

* ensures that each member of the group has clearly defined targets for improving performance,

* plugs any gaps in the abilities of the group by training and development,

* constantly evaluates results and monitors progress towards the goals.

(b) *Getting the best out of each individual*

He will see that each person,

* gets a sense of personal achievement in his job,

* feels he is making a worthwhile contribution,

* if his performance is unsatisfactory is told in what way and given help to improve,

* feels that his job challenges him and his capabilities are matched by the responsibilities given him,

* receives adequate recognition for his achievements, etc., etc.

(c) *Keeping high group morale*

The leader,

* provides regular opportunities for briefing the group,

* provides regular opportunities for genuine consultations before reaching decision affecting them,

* accords the official representative of the group the facilities he needs to be its effective spokesman,

* ensures that there is a formal and fair grievance procedure understood by all, etc.

And what of the 'man' who is managed, or rather 'led'? Here again, there is little ambiguity. The man who is properly managed simply loves it. His life fills with meaning and he realizes that this was his destiny: he was born to be managed and, if his turn comes, to move on to managing others. The cycle turns by itself, without any questions being asked of the institutional disposition of power containing it. Hence Smith's list of 'the sort of comments' that might be made about a respected leader:

He is human and treats us as human beings.

Doesn't bear grudges; has no favourites; is fair to us as well as the company.

He is easy to talk to and he listens – you can tell he listens.

He is honest; keeps his word; doesn't dodge unpleasant issues.

Drives himself hard – you don't mind him expecting best of you.
(Smith, p. 32)

The picture scarcely needs elaboration. Management has been defined as a set of functions which are designed to create an inclusive and enthusiastically productive atmosphere, while at the same time reinforcing and overhauling the structures of power. 'Consultation', for example, must be 'genuine', but under no circumstances must it challenge the authority of the leader: decision-making power remains absolutely with the manager, although his decisions stand to be informed and also legitimated by the 'consultation' process (small wonder most 'joint consultation' meetings between management and staff are preoccupied with trivia – issues like the tea machine). The most productive atmosphere may be informal, and lacking in displayed differences (like separate canteens for managers and directors). But with the line of authority clearly defined as ever, informality only goes to show that managerial power and hier-archical command structures are benign and effective, in the interests of all. Similarly, the development of 'team-spirit', or even corporate identity, might suggest a certain kind of solidarity, but people are still individually accountable for their 'tasks', and any failure of 'performance' is only sharpened by the extent to which it might be claimed that in this informal and 'participative' atmosphere, the very targets which have been missed were 'agreed' by the person now facing disciplinary action. Adair and his followers may talk about getting results 'through' people, but the results are what really count, and the sales pitch never ceases to stress that this kind of leadership makes for better work and greater profits. As these specialists in banality and cliché also say, 'He who communicates is he who leads.' 'Communication' becomes a euphemism for 'control'.

What is to be made of this mixture of motivation theory, boy heroism, humanistic psychology and confident as well as dissembling pragmatism? The point we want to stress here is that this mixture is humanistic in more than emphasis or rhetoric. While it certainly dresses up organizational power in humanistic clothes, this conception of management also goes beyond any matter of disguise. It is premised on an image of the personality, or of what it is to be a person at work, in which people recognize and identify themselves to a considerable extent. In other words, it works according to a certain view of human nature, and makes its offers to people (the managed as well as managers) accordingly. People need to belong to a group, they need recognition, they are competitive, they crave meaning and like to be informed or asked for their views, they can be 'handled' if you approach them in the right way first, they can motivate and discipline themselves, they do not always put money first, etc.

Much more than this, we are not just dealing with a vague and free floating 'theory' of human nature with which everyone must consciously agree. This theory is practically and concretely installed in the experience of work – thus, for example, there are regular 'briefing' groups to ensure that a managerial view of 'communication' and 'motivation' enters the practice of work. In short, there is a management practice or technique for every vital aspect of the theory, and the theory consequently becomes 'operational' as a routine and concrete reality, not just as a set of ideas.

The managerial technology of 'excellence'

If Adair typifies a view of management which has been widely held in Britain since the sixties, there have been some loud trumpetings recently from America which announce yet another new theory of management for the eighties – new insights, new ideas, revelations for those who really want to blast on through. All this and more is offered in *In Search of Excellence*, a book by Thomas Peters and Robert Waterman, Junior, both of whom are – or have been – connected with McKinsey, one of the largest and most influential of multi-national business consultancy firms.[6]

For Peters and Waterman, whose book has been widely read in the United States and also in management circles in Britain, it all comes down to what they call 'excellence'. 'Excellence' has been taken up as a keyword in a welter of related strategies aimed at shoring up an establishment threatened by a wide variety of insistent and untidily democratic demands for participation. It has seemed recently to be the fate of Excellence to be championed by the mediocre in the interests of the worst. But even in this situation there have been limits. It is therefore to the distinction, if not un-ambiguously the credit, of Thomas Peters and Robert Waterman, Junior, that they should finally have chased Excellence down to a new roost. After a long search they've found it at McDonald's, in amongst all those child workers and hamburgers.

In Search of Excellence is sub-titled 'Lessons from America's Best-run Companies', although it would be more accurate to call it 'Lessons from American Multinationals' since these, almost without exception, are the companies they discuss (there is also an almost exclusive emphasis on productive organizations rather than those, say, in the financial services field). It is a book which zips along in a style which is both fast and carefully laid back, full of groomed testosterone and that curious blend of machismo and zen which (after the defeat in Vietnam and the rise of OPEC) stands as the hallmark of a newly modified type of American success – one that became clearly visible during the Carter administration. We speak of style, although this is more like a kind of interior design of the mind in which that habitual and driving assertiveness encounters a new sense of paradox (if not anything so shocking as a direct sense of limitation).

Insights don't simply fall from the air for these authors. They seem more likely to spring from the plush-piled carpets of expensive hotels and board rooms around the world. They might also be gleaned over a drink with clients, perhaps, or strike as one cuts a path (a lean and deodorized figure in a sharp suit?) across some airport departure lounge. But there can be no doubt that the best route to the heart of the matter in this world of semi-theorized pragmatism is to get right down to it with some successful man – some 'pathbreaker' – in shirtsleeves. What did he do? What turned him on? What made a 'champion' of this mortal American? For Peters and Waterman what matters is 'a workforce that's turned on', and more particularly what they call 'the "high" of being an American worker'. All this stuff about Japanese management techniques (we're talking about the post-Hiroshima/Nagasaki economic miracle with its 'quality circles' – workers who gather *voluntarily* to discuss possible improvements in performance – and related management paraphernalia) evidently needs beating back a bit. Americans can cut the mustard (this is an IBM phrase) as enthusiastically as anyone, but 'if America is to regain its competitive position in the world', then we'd certainly better move on past Weber as well, that figure from a tired old continent who 'pooh-poohed' charisma.

If *In Search of Excellence* is written in swaggering prose and high-tech jargon, its authors do not distinguish themselves by any excessive displays of modesty in their self-presentation, either. They acknowledge the special contribution of one David Anderson, a junior at McKinsey, whose 'awesome intellectual prowess' and 'dogged intellectual pursuit of key ideas' was clearly of considerable help to them as they put these pages together (books like this are never exactly written). As for their own contribution to management thinking, they measure this in the understated terms of 'quantum steps' as they deal with those 'hunks of complexity' which they consider to lie at the core of organizational experience. As they saunter through the weird bazaar of 'management theory' ('Studies show that the right half of the brain is great at visualising things but can't verbalise any of them' . . . etc.), they announce themselves to be among the real makers, fellow technicians of nothing less than a paradigm shift (Kuhn, of course, boils down to a snappy summary sentence or two). Thanks to this Copernican shift we can now hear James Watson describing the double-helix – 'It's so beautiful, you see, so beautiful' – and then move on to Ray Kroc, founder – or rather chief pirate – of MacDonald's and gifted architect of the Big Mac, as he marvels over the beauty which he claims to find in the hamburger bun. New ground indeed and, as these purveyors of 'leading-edge theory' say in their claimed departure from the tradition of Taylor (Mayo's famous Hawthorne studies were 'just a bunch of straightforward studies of industrial hygiene factors'), 'we believe we are breaking some important theoretical ground here.'

But despite the grandiose claims of *In Search of Excellence*, the paradigm with which Peters and Waterman rest is not essentially different from that of Adair – the aims and conditions of business are taken for granted the same. Nevertheless, this book does oppose the idea of the organization as a united entity steered by a single focus of power and decision-making at the top. For Peters and Waterman, management is not – whatever rationalistic accountants may want it to be – a simple process of control, but rather the active *integration* of multiple and diverse decision-making processes. Of course, power remains, but Peters and Waterman approach their multinationals with a view to unfreezing them, galvanizing them into a greater diversity and creativity (recent shocks to these Goliaths have included the challenge of little 'champions' like the people who came up with Apple Computers – a new threat from the suburban garage or basement and an organization which has gone on to assert its 'non-managerial' style of organization). Their book comes from a milieu in which everyone is now talking about organizational 'tents' and 'temporary structures', rather than fixed and consolidated forms, and in which the idea of a shadow structure alongside the formal hierarchy is considered increasingly valuable and useful, rather than threatening. In these terms the good multinational is said to be the one which behaves as if it were an open range with its staff camped out like cowboys around scattered fires. It has also been advocated, and not just by Peters and Waterman, that big organizations should foster internal competition, asking their staff to work as 'intra-preneurs' who tender for bits of work in teams of their own making – this way, so the theory goes, things will be done cheaper and the workforce will be even more 'turned on' than usual. We've had wheels within wheels for long enough, so why not try jungles within jungles? The good monolith, then, is the one which works flexibly and non-bureaucratically, constantly unfreezing itself as it goes along. The successful company – the one which makes profits – is the one which takes money almost for granted rather than letting ac-countants dictate every measure; it is the one which takes risks rather than following immobilizing, if supposedly foolproof, rationalistic strategies calculated years ahead of time.

If developing a *'bias for action'* (often at the expense of analysis) is the first attribute of 'Excellence' in Peters and Waterman, what are the others? There is being *Close to the Customer* (providing a good service, listening to customers, treating them as a likely source of new product ideas). Then there is a stress on *Autonomy and Entrepreneur-ship* (the fostering of leaders, innovators and champions means not holding people on a short rein); on *Productivity through People* (treat the rank and file as the 'root source' of quality – and make unions unnecessary: against the collectivist approach, follow IBM in its claimed respect for the individual). Then there is the importance of being *Hands-on and Value-driven* (the good manager is on the spot; great leaders or 'champions' are legendary for 'walking the plant floors', or what the Industrial Society calls 'the job'). After this comes *Stick to the Knitting* (conglomerates are a drag; specialize and build on what you know) and then the importance of *Simple form, Lean staff* (the structure should be simple and unambiguous, with not too many people at the top; uncomplicated authority – definitely not complex matrix arrangements – is best and even most 'elegant'). Finally, the excellent company is said to have *Simultaneous loose-tight properties* (the excellent companies are both centralized and decentralized – fanatical about central points and core values, but flexible elsewhere).

Perhaps the centre of all this, however, concerns meaning. Culture has been on the map as an issue in American business for some time now, and there are even consultancy companies with names like 'Oral History Associates' which specialize in the derivation of corporate myths and meanings.[7] For Peters and Waterman this is absolutely the way forward. They even say that business should start learning from the liberal arts (whoops, pity about all those cuts in the Universities!). In this view IBM has culture, and not in the sense that Armand Mattelart means when he writes about IBM's endeavours to control and manipulate Third World culture.[8] Peters and Waterman aren't about to start thinking about *those* particular cultural strategies. Their point is that IBM has an internal culture, a pervasive sense of what it is and where it is going which can inform the self-understanding of its employees. With staff already hooked into the Corporation as subjects of these values, then of course respect for the 'individual' can be tantamount. It also poses no threat whatsoever. Meaning, therefore, becomes a major management resource. It underlies the turned-on workforce.

Of course there is no paradigm shift here. The new truths are actually home-truths of Adair's sort, and these home-truths are tricks to keep the boat on course. As Adair says in answer to unionist Frank Cousins who claimed in 1964 that there were two purposes in industry, 'We must firmly reject this viewpoint as a perceptual distortion of the three-circle model.' By now Adair has moved on to become Professor of 'Leadership Studies' at the University of Surrey. It would probably not be very interesting to know how such a chair came to be endowed. After all, and as Professor Adair, who apparently also runs a private consultancy, says to the unions, the 'non-monetary' aspects of work are so much more important.

Turning the questions around

Why shouldn't we just laugh contemptuously? Why, when we turn the questions back on ourselves, do the habitual sneer and the disillusioning perspectives of the jaundiced eye seem inadequate? The first reason is surely to be found in the fact that this 'operationalized' theory of human motivation and behaviour actually *works* to such a large extent, and not just in the crude sense of being efficient. The point is rather that while these management thinkers peddle a view of humanity which is full of self-seeking, machismo and egoism, they also provide a version of solidarity, advocate a limited form of personal authority, and never cease to stress the importance of providing staff with a sense of purpose and meaning which evidently *can* 'turn people on'. If Peters and Waterman eventually discover a simple elegance in the hierarchy once it has been cleared of all that accountant-led hesitancy and bureaucracy, their organizational Reaganism should be understood for more than the fact that it takes us towards the brave new post-union world, in which no-one need even notice the distant exploitation which forms the underside of so much multi-national 'Excellence'. For, along with its many carefully laid silences, this reinstatement of assertive and competitive corporate culture, with its 'team-based' command structures, also works by coopting some of the best aspects of what is still widely experienced as human nature – something only a fool, or an arrogant fantasist of revolution, would write off as nothing. People can find a place for themselves in this picture, and for significant numbers of people the experience of work is definitely not just the hellish routine of enforced labour. This attachment to the managed organization of work clearly has its limits, but we are certainly unlikely to understand these limits unless the degree of responsiveness and acquiescence in people's relationship to managerial practice is considered with some respect. There can be no future in invoking an abstract idea of 'the worker' to justify ignoring the way millions of people are positively, if also ambivalently, engaged in their work, managed as it is.

The second reason why the jaundiced eye is not to be trusted concerns its false assumption that all management activity and thinking is identical as an expression of class interests. To dismiss all management theory and practice as a set of tricks which are identical with the general interest of a ruling class is inadequate for many reasons. As Jim Tomlinson has argued, organizations are not merely transparent crystallizations of wider social relations already formed elsewhere (e.g., classes, whether ruling or working), and the fact that 'management' changes and can follow a variety of different forms and strategies certainly indicates that management's ideas and practices are not frozen into a simple identity with capitalist interests.[9] There is also a vital distinction to be made between 'management' as those people who hold managerial positions, and 'management', as an assortment of integrative functions which are necessary in any complex organization – planning, harmonizing related processes, ensuring appropriate flows of information, matching resources to production needs, marketing, financial control, linking output and demand, etc. Functions of this sort will be necessary in any kind of organization, capitalist or otherwise.

None of this is to say that management as practised, or as advocated by many consultants, is not harnessed to a capitalist regime or that it lies in any way beyond criticism. Our point, instead, is that the habitual sneer seems to be more a form of *denial* than of criticism. How far has the sneer taken us? It has certainly indicated how ideas of management are scarcely theoretical in coherence at all, but rather cobbled together out of all sorts of rags and tatters which are then flaunted as 'science' or 'knowledge'. It has indicated the extent to which dominant suppositions about management scrupulously avoid raising any political or ethical questions about organizational regime – indeed, their function is often limited to precisely the obscuring of these questions. It has indicated how management practice denies real autonomy to people while at the same time offering them comfort, understanding, therapy and even the culture of corporate myths and meaning.

But if these points are well made, the sneer also persists in reducing all organizational practice and experience to a wider and abstract opposition between generally conceived interests. And from this standpoint it is impossible to define (or even notice) the real concrete particularities of decision-making within organizations or of their standing vis-a-vis the market, the various practices of the finance system or even, in some cases, of their funding bodies. Only where a more adequate understanding of organizational management exists will it be possible to define ways of carrying out management functions in a more genuinely democratic way. Thus, if there is a need to get beyond simplifying myths of leadership, command and the single organizational objective, such as we find in Adair and (differently phrased) Peters and Waterman, many myths on the left – including the retarding beliefs that there can be no worthwhile reform at the level of the individual organization without a wider social revolution and that the division of labour is simply to be eradicated – also need to be dismantled.[10]

An understanding of organizational management is badly needed on the left. We should be defining management not as crude power or authority, but as the *relative* authority which is needed if complex tasks are to be carried out efficiently – a *relative* authority which can surely itself be managed so that it is accountable to the whole. Similarly, we should be thinking of hierarchy not just as a fixed and instituted power relation, but as a way of patterning and organizing activity which will include authority and expertise, but which can be used in a temporary, mobile and accountable way to achieve specific social and political objectives. Likewise, instead of just sneering at rationalized notions of efficiency, we should be asking what are our own criteria of organizational *effectiveness*, and what are the priorities according to which we decide what is possible and what must be given up for the sake of something more important. If we need to think of management as an integrative process and to define its functions as they apply to particular organizations (and of course they will be different from one organization to the next), there is obviously no point in doing this in a way that merely reinvents the semi-expert role of 'manager'. Indeed, an understanding of management needs to be widely shared within organizations, precisely so that management functions can be carried out in an accountable way, even when they do demand specific skills and expertise which not everyone in the organization will necessarily possess.

Finally, we are in no doubt at all, there is a lot to be learned from management thinking. We would hardly advocate uncritical conformity to these ideas, but there is scarcely an area of necessary management activity in which orthodox views are *completely* beside the point.

Chapter VI

Where do we go from here?

In this section we try to spell out some of the implications of our critique of libertarian attitudes to business and organization. In effect, we are trying to set down one or two 'pointers' as to organizational problems that groups are likely to encounter and, where possible, to make some suggestions as to useful ways to approach these problems.

We have noticed that organizational difficulties come up persistently in relation to three issues:

(a) the 'stage of life' of a project

(b) the size of the group – i.e., numbers of people involved, and

(c) the particular function of the organization (e.g., campaigning, service-provision, self-help, etc.).

We will take each of these in turn.

(a) 'Stage of life'

Crudely, organizations do have a life-cycle – they usually start small, grow at a greater or lesser speed, plateau for a while and then fade away or die off. This banal observation actually has important consequences. In short, it's worth thinking about the types of changes that an organization is likely to go through over time, and the kinds of problems that these transitions are likely to throw up.

In recent years the world of management consultancy has had a lot to say about the inevitability of 'change', and the management 'challenge' which it poses. In these cases 'change' means redundancy, new technology, rationalization, etc. The word is a buzz word for 'fate' – 'change' is something that happens to people, and almost invariably its impact is negative. In this situation the very idea of 'change' becomes suspect. Nevertheless, changes do happen and often need to be encouraged. An intelligent and deliberate conception of change will lie at the heart of any alert and democratic organization. The key point is that those affected by change should be involved in the process of decision-making. Change will be necessary as, for instance, a group grows from being a small circle of friends to being a national network of sub-groups. If this kind of change is not registered in a new organizational structure and self-understanding, disaster lurks round the corner. Indeed, while the need for a change of organizational form may often be a mark of the original group's success in having produced a project which has outgrown its initial basis, unmanaged change of this sort can bring about the most violent and destructive kinds of collapse.

Nevertheless, it is a common experience that those originally involved in setting up a group or project find it hard to let go of the levers of control at a later stage, especially when the group has had (as it often does), one or more 'charismatic' figure(s), who have been vital to its success in the early period. Such people are usually heavily identified with the project and regard it as, in some sense, 'their baby'. Often, in this situation, progress through the deadlock which ensues is only possible by means of some kind of 'ritual slaughter' of the original 'Father(s)' or 'Mother(s)' of the group, to make room for the new entrants to take on some real responsibility for the direction of the project. The original people can only successfully block this at the cost of the decline and decay of the organization itself. It should be said that voluntary, 'caring', or politically enlightened organizations can often be just as brutal in these situations as commercial companies. Indeed, they can be uniquely vicious.

Particular ways of working can only be sustained for a given period. For example, a campaigning group of highly committed unemployed young graduates can probably work 12 hours a day, seven days a week, for very little pay, for up to six months, running, presumably, on their commitment and enthusiasm. They will not be able to sustain this kind of activity indefinitely, and if the campaign needs to exist over a longer period, it will be necessary to reduce the working hours and increase the pay for them to sustain it. Moreover, it would be absurd to expect all the people who get involved in the campaign at a later stage, with varying degrees of commitment, to 'live up to' the high-pressure standards set in the campaign's launch period.

Equally, where a group is wishing to expand and 'open up' its activities from operating within a given social network, to attracting people from varying backgrounds, it will usually be necessary to change the conditions of membership (or terms of employment) in order to accommodate varying interests and expectations. Otherwise the group will, in effect, remain 'closed' – in the sense of being open only to people from a particular social background who share the original members' cultural predispositions.

Transitions of this sort are more or less inevitable and

organizations are more likely to be able to steer a way through them if this is understood from the beginning.

Whatever form of organization you start with, it should always be understood as provisional – the most appropriate to the circumstances of the time – and subject to modification as and when necessary, rather than being held sacrosanct as the original, and therefore 'authentic' and unchangeable form of organization for all time, and in all circumstances. If this sort of understanding is to exist within the organization as it goes along, the process of reflection and self-examination are structurally essential.

(b) Size

One determining factor in the way you choose to run an organization is size. To make an obvious statement, you cannot run a large steel mill as a collective. However, up to 4 – 6 people can probably choose to function quite effectively in all areas as a collective. Above that number, a much clearer allocation of responsibilities is needed, with different people having different specialist tasks. This will usually involve the recognition of the need for management as a function, and it will often require individuals to be responsible for managing the work of others. Although there is no clearly agreed 'rule of thumb', there will be a limit to the number of people (about 10) whose work can be effectively coordinated through one person, depending on the complexity of task involved and the amount of personal contact that people are able to sustain.

Another crucial factor, which is related to size, is the relative proportions of those carrying out core activities and those doing the back-up or administrative work.

Often campaigning organizations prioritize what they see as 'action' over the development of an adequate administrative base, without realizing that for large-scale campaigning activity to be effective and democratic there must be proper administrative back-up. In the analogy much loved by management theorists, this is like the relationship between the fighting part of an army and its logistical part – which provides the food and supplies to fight with. If immediate action is glorified in this way, administration will always appear as a hindering and petty bureaucracy, and thus will always be seen in a negative light.

The same basic problem crops up in product and service-oriented enterprises, in another form: here it is the question of the relative number of those employed to carry out sales and marketing, as against those employed to produce products or services. Thus, a printing cooperative will often take on more print-shop workers when it should really be putting a 'rep.' on the road to market its services.

(c) Function

Both in the field of cultural practice and the field of organizational politics we have too often erected a one-dimensional model of 'Good Practice' quite independently of the demands of our particular, and varied, circumstances and their differing requirements. We spoke earlier of the need to create an organizational typology – of the different forms of organization which might be best suited to different circumstances. One simple starting point would be the three-part typology of 'mutual aid', 'user-based' and 'campaigning organizations'. This typology (which we borrow from Charles Handy) is approximate and we don't offer it as a closed model, but the main point is that there are different styles of organization appropriate to different objectives; and that unnecessary confusion will result when an organizational form which is appropriate to one type of activity is generalized across all the others.[1] Thus, for example, Des Wilson, campaigner extraordinaire, has recently suggested that the very idea of unions in voluntary organizations is a depressing aberration – as if people should be happy to work day and night for peanuts and the cause.[2] This approach may be acceptable in a situation where the project is short-term and the labour is voluntary – and this sacrifice may be the condition of belonging to the elect of those who are saved. But applied to organizations in which people are employed to do particular jobs, this way of thinking would be simply grotesque. Indeed, it would be no better than the worst philanthropic perspective: as this is a caring organization, our staff can be expected to slave for nothing. Surely it must be possible to create an organizational culture in which workers don't ritualistically count their hours without detracting from the rights of employees to decent terms of employment.

(i) Mutual aid organizations

This type of organization needs no elaborate structure. It scarcely needs a policy and is unlikely to have any executive function. It is concerned only with its members' own satisfaction, is not tied to any external timetable of demands and, thus, has no need to develop the ability to take decisions or to act quickly. It is not necessarily concerned with efficiency, in so far as it is not attempting to produce any good or service other than that of mutual satisfaction.

The great bulk of 'front-room' organizations (such as babysitting circles, study groups, self-help groups formed, say, by parents of children with a particular handicap) fall into this category. Clearly, these kinds of autonomous small organizations are very effective as ways in which people can cooperate to help each other. The problems start either when there is an attempt to make a national federation out of a number of such groups, or when the organizational looseness which is appropriate to this form is transposed to a context where those involved are trying to produce goods or services for external consumption. If, for example, a mutual aid group for parents of handicapped children starts to run a school, a new style of organization will need to be agreed and adopted in full awareness of the changes entailed.

(ii) User-based organizations

By this we mean organizations running a wholefood shop, or a telephone advice service, or producing a magazine – any case in which the organization is producing goods or services for external consumption. Such an organization will need to separate policy formation from executive action. In other words, it is going to have to decide what its strategic priorities are and work out tactically how it is going to achieve them. It will need to be concerned with both efficiency and effectiveness (i.e., the magazine has to come out by a certain date, someone needs to open the shop at a given time, etc.) in a way that mutual aid organizations are not. It will also need to be concerned with its relations to its users, establishing forms of feedback and so on.

(iii) Campaigning

The charismatic 'individualist' is liable to have a central place here (especially in the launch phase of a campaign, whereas elsewhere s/he is likely to be a pain in the arse). A great emphasis on flexibility and tactics (rather than general fixed policy) is likely – i.e., the organization may need to be able to respond fast enough to refigure itself totally in 24 hours, as its campaign develops to a 'crisis point'. It will need to be concerned with attracting, motivating and mobilizing its members and developing an effective lobbying policy. In the case of small short-life campaigns, much of the labour will be done by volunteers, and everyone involved is likely to be overstretched and overstrained. In the case of the larger, long-term campaigning organizations, a degree of bureaucracy and institutionalization will be necessary in order to maintain the activity over the longer term.;

Clearly, this three-part typology of organizations is laughably simple, but it at least begins the work of defining organizational horses in relation to different kinds of courses – and without a recognition of such differences we can only continue to flounder. While further development of this typology would certainly be useful, working through the relations between an organization's external goals and its internal structure, the sketch we have provided should indicate how much confusion can follow when organizational forms appropriate to one type of purpose are carried over unawares into a situation where a different orientation exists. These, for instance, are indeed among the classic management problems of the voluntary and campaigning sector.

Recurring issues in organization

Having now sketched in our observations about the different organizational solutions which may be appropriate to different circumstances, we now offer some thoughts on a set of key issues which, in our experience, have come up again and again in different groups and in different contexts. These issues are:

1. Authority, leadership and direction,

2. Working relations,

3. External and internal objectives,

4. Organizational culture and motivation,

5. Flexibility and innovation.

We will take these in turn:

1. Authority, leadership and direction
In management circles, as we have seen, it is commonplace to discuss questions of authority under the rubric of 'leadership'. Here the emphasis usually falls on the personal qualities of the much-vaunted leader 'himself'. In this way everything becomes a matter of either finding the superior being or of generalizing 'his' abilities or 'skills' which can be passed on to lower mortals in expensive training courses. Perhaps it is understandable that the world of co-ops and collectives has shied away from all this. But, in rejecting the mystifying cult of leadership, one shouldn't then ignore questions of authority and direction which are essential to much organizational activity. In our view, authority can be relative rather than absolute, accountable rather than a law unto itself, an organizational tool rather than a rigidified and unquestioned hierarchy. It can be agreed,

granted, evaluated and changed.

As for direction, this doesn't necessarily have to come down to the sayings of the boss, but has to do with intelligence in assessing options, defining possibilities in relation to changing circumstances, and in providing a basis on which people can move forward coherently. If we extend this argument to the question of leadership, our main point is that while the cult of the personal leader may certainly be dispensed with, certain activities and functions of leadership and direction are vital.

Beyond the generalized predilection for cooperative and collective forms of organization and job-rotation which has characterized the radical movements in this country over the last few years, there is one specific notion which is shared by nearly all groups. This is the rejection of the idea that groups need leaders. While we, too, are happy to agree that groups do not necessarily need leaders, as such (i.e., a specific person or persons with the exclusive formal power and responsibility to order other people about), we do believe that groups need leadership and direction. It is a matter of disentangling the essential function at issue from the particular cultural forms with which it has come to be associated in commercial organizations.

The clearest exposition of this argument that we have found is by Bruce Kokopeli and George Lakey. As they put it:[3]

'Having experienced the worst forms of leadership, many of us... declared leadership to be bankrupt. We attempted to form and run 'leaderless' groups. The groups often fell apart quickly; where they held together it was because leadership was in fact exerted, but in a hidden way so that no one knew quite what was happening...

We didn't see the very crucial difference between leaders and leadership; between the *role* and the *functions* of leadership'

Leadership, as a function or direction, is simply the use of either authority or influence within a group to help it achieve its goals. Thought about in this way, any group member trying to influence others in the group, is attempting to exercise leadership – and that is a vital function for the group's survival and success. It is vital for as wide as possible a section of the membership to be prepared to take on the responsibilities involved in acting this way, rather than to wait on someone else to 'show the way'.

This clearly involves the recognition of power and of people being prepared to take the responsibilities that go with power. Here it is not enough simply to have a democratic decision-making process – left at that point one has avoided the crucial question of the power to set the agenda of decisions that have to be made. Again, Kokopeli and Lakey put the point well:

'Democratic decision-making is not enough. Decision-making is an inflexible exercise of power after the terms are set: the structure designates who can make what decisions under what circumstances. Leadership, on the other hand, is a flexible use of power to influence other group members, thereby formulating the terms in which the decision is made. In addition to democratic decision-making, therefore, we need democratic or shared leadership.' *(p. 13)*

The point about leadership and direction is that, whether one takes Adair's list of functions which a 'good leader' performs, or Kokopeli and Lakey's list of goal achievement (or task functions) and group maintenance objectives (or morale functions), leadership as a function is simply necessary if a group is to achieve its goals, maintain itself as a group in good working order, and adapt to changes in its environment. One may safely reject the notion of groups needing leaders, but to reject the notion of groups needing leadership is self-defeating.

2. Working relations: money and rights

Any organization needs to be clear about its decision-making structures. It needs to be clear how policy is established, by whom, and what degrees of independence are to be allowed, to whom, in the implementation of policy. While we are certainly not of the view that there is one right way to resolve these questions, there can be little doubt that they need to be thought through and settled in procedures that are both agreed and understood by everyone.

In these discussions, certain themes are likely to come up again and again. Thus, for example, some types of decisions can only be made to work if they are agreed by consensus – e.g., the decision to employ a new person in a small organization, where everyone needs to get along well for the good of the organization. Secondly, there are some issues which can be settled by vote (e.g., should people be allowed to smoke in the office) and, thirdly, those matters that rightly lie within the relative authority of people with particular agreed responsibilities and experience (e.g., should the organization use printer X or printer Y to produce its leaflets). Similarly, it needs to be clear that some decisions are so routine or trivial that they shouldn't even come to a meeting at all. Indeed, the appearance of such routine issues on the agenda for a meeting is often a sign that something is badly wrong within the organization.

If these kinds of question are resolved, or at least made explicit within the public discussions of the organization, then other issues are far less likely to cause problems. Thus, for example, it should be possible to resolve the painful dichotomy that arises in many collective organizations between the asserted autonomy of the organization itself and the desire for privacy on the part of members who find their private lives being scrutinized and judged by their work colleagues. Similarly, the difficulties many organizations experience in defining the limits to positive discrimination can be traced back to a lack of clarity over their key objectives and priorities.

One of the rallying cries around which people in this sector have gathered over the last few years is 'Equal-Pay-for-All'. Unfortunately, there are a number of difficulties with this policy which have often bedevilled attempts to implement it. At its simplest, it can be said that it is a policy which can only be applied easily in a limited range of situations. It works well if the employees have all agreed to work for a (self-exploiting) wage well below the market rate.

The problem is that having to set the wage at such a low level, through the familiar straitened circumstances, is effectively an *unequal* opportunities policy: only certain types of people (e.g., those below a certain age, those without dependents) will be able to afford to work for such low wages. Moreover, the group will always be in danger of losing its most 'valuable' workers who, if they are being paid well below the 'market rate' for their work, may in the end be tempted to go off and work elsewhere.

Alternatively, equal pay works well if there is enough money to pay everyone at the market wage of those employees who would command the highest wage on the open market. The problem here is that everyone else will be being 'overpaid' by definition (compared with market rates), which will mean that it's very hard for the group's products to be competitive in the market, as compared with the products of groups without an equal pay system; therefore the project is likely to have a greater financial struggle.

Moreover, there are fundamental difficulties with the notion of equal pay itself. Thus, it's hard to see how equal pay is in fact equitable – as between single people and those with dependents. Fairness can only then be achieved by linking pay, on a sliding scale, to need, rather than opting for arithmetical 'equality' of all wages. But, then, what of those who have other 'special' needs (the disabled, those who need a special diet, etc.)? How do we define what is to count as a 'special need'.

Beyond these difficulties about the distribution of wages there are the further difficulties of how to distribute financial resources as between wages (in toto) and (re)investment in the project itself. Thus, for instance, there may well be differences within an organization between those who are most highly committed to the long-term welfare of the organization (and are thus liable to prioritize reinvestment of any surplus in the project) and those for whom it is simply the provider of a relatively short-term job (and who are thus likely to prefer to take out any surplus in the form of higher wages). In other circumstances there may be a conflict between those who see the external political objectives of the project as the primary thing and are, therefore, prepared to work for very low wages to subsidise the project, and those who are more concerned about the internal work conditions (who may wish to prioritise funding maternity/paternity leave and other social benefits for the staff).

Often those who espouse collective working and equal pay avoid the problem of creating obvious inequalities within their organization by locating the inequality somewhere else. For example, when the South East London Consortium decided to become a collective, everyone agreed to do their own typing so that no one would have to be 'serviced' by someone else. However, as one of the workers honestly admitted,[4] the problem did not go away:

'The question of temporary typists was slightly more complex. Frequently in the past we had hired the services of a professional typist when, for example, a lengthy report had to be produced. We recognized that there were potential dangers in coming to rely on this as a solution to work overload for the rest of us and, to, as it were, admit "servicing" workers by the back door. Nevertheless, we agreed in the end that it was all right to buy outside typists' time for exceptional, one-off jobs, provided we paid them the commercial hourly going rate for this and regarded them not as temporary workers, but as outside contractors like, for instance, printers, plumbers or, indeed, cleaners.'

If collectives can export their problems with their more boring work to outsiders, other difficulties derive from the fact that those people who have been most committed to democratic working have, by and large, been well-educated, middle-class people who have a long-term commitment to working in this way (and who are also likely to reap career benefits at a later stage from having 'served their time' on a good cause in this way). The kind of organizations they create, with often absolutist positions about commitment and ideals, do not allow any space for successfully employing working-class people who often regard work more simply as a 'job' which they have agreed to do (and whose 'career prospects' are of a quite different kind). Unless we can create forms of organization which can also satisfy the needs of those who view work as 'just a job', those who work democratically will always remain a self-enclosed, middle-class group, a semi-religious order, who have in fact successfully left the 'inequalities' they wished to tackle fundamentally unchanged.

Any organization must have clear rules on hiring and firing and promotion and demotion. It is important to be clear about what the organization wants people to do (a clear job description is essential) and what competence any person interviewed will need to have. Any policy of positive discrimination has to ensure that it functions to discriminate positively between two people who are qualified to do the job, unless there is a specific policy to provide on-the-job training for people who have the desired social characteristics but lack the necessary skills. Only in this way can we avoid the difficulty one agency known to us experienced, when they took on a particular person under a particular category for reasons of positive discrimination. As that person did not possess the necessary qualifications to do the job competently and the group had failed to provide adequate in-service training, the agency's reputation suffered disastrously as bad advice and service was given to people who could not afford to be advised badly.

3. External and internal objectives

Throughout this document we have talked about effectiveness. This is not merely a polite way of invoking the idea of efficiency. 'Efficiency' is part of the rhetoric of business culture and is therefore too narrow and loaded in its implications for our purposes. But while we can reject the notion of efficiency, this obviously does not mean that we abandon all interest in how well things are done. Effectiveness is about getting results, but it also takes into account the culture of the organization and its constituency, which goes beyond purely material considerations. In this sense an 'efficient' practice can be ineffective in that it cuts against the motivating principles of an organization and thus achieves short-term results only at the expense of engendering long-term difficulties for the organization.

It must be part of an organization's responsibility to determine its own criteria of effectiveness and this discussion must obviously involve as many of the group's members as necessary. The organization's members need to be clear, both about what their organization's external purposes are (e.g., getting a new pedestrian crossing, raising the level of public consciousness about acid rain, etc.) and how these are going to be achieved (staging a demonstration, starting a newsletter?). This, of course, will involve further calculations about whether the group has the resources (money, skill, time, etc.) necessary to achieve these objectives, and about what the internal consequences of using these methods (arrest, exhaustion, bankruptcy?) will be for the organization.

In short, it will be necessary to think hard both about the external and internal dimensions of the group's work, and to develop mechanisms for reconciling the conflicts that will inevitably arise between, for example, the need to produce an efficient service or an effective campaign and the group's members' needs for good working conditions. What might be a good idea, in the short term, for external purposes (e.g., running a 24-hour telephone advice service) may be a bad idea, in the long term, for internal reasons. In this example we could reasonably hypothesize that the internal consequences of running such a demanding service would be that everyone in the group would get exhausted, and staff turnover would be so high as to make it hard for the group to maintain any sense of coherence and continuity, quite apart from the fact that high staff turnover will mean that no-one is around long enough to become skilled, and thus the 'product' (i.e., the advice) will tend to be of a poor quality.

It will be necessary to clarify who the external constituency is, on behalf of (or with) whom the group is working, or for whom the service or product is being provided. Who are they? Where are they? How many of them are there? How close are the group's links to them? How effective are the mechanisms of 'feedback' between the members of the organization and the wider group with whom it is trying to work? Does the group 'listen' to external responses to its work? What mechanisms exist to ensure that this happens? Does the group know the state of current thinking (about it and its works) 'out there'? Clearly, it is vital to build and maintain these kinds of links. A project that fails to do so has little chance of long-term survival. Indeed, splitting your organization from its community/users/ clients and environment is a sure recipe for disaster.

Implicit in this argument is the importance of maintaining the external effectiveness of your work, so as to be able to recognize when you're failing, and to adjust policy accordingly. Given how few resources projects often have, it's clearly foolish to risk squandering them on policies that are, for whatever reason, failing to have the external impact they were supposed to have. Used in this way, monitoring and feedback can enable you to learn from your failures before they become terminal.

Monitoring will also be necessary internally. Again, given scarce resources, a project will need to monitor the effectiveness of its work. This will mean defining criteria according to which competence, efficiency and failure can be assessed. Targets will need to be set so that people can get a clear sense of how far short of achieving objectives they're falling at any given moment, and some form of sanctions on ineffectiveness (whether moral disapproval, dismissal or being shot at dawn) will need to be developed and agreed. Often the need for this sort of evaluation gets lost in the business of satisfying external funding – evaluation becomes a cosmetic prelude to the next round of grant applications. But the wide-spread reluctance to monitor or evaluate reflects more than personal incompetence. Organizations have secrets. Genuine evaluation means making explicit the (often contradictory) premises on which the organization exists. An organization that says it is meeting social needs may well be reluctant to accept that it is also thriving on those needs; or that its programme of activity also functions to meet the organization's need to survive – by proving that there are social needs in the community and, therefore, a need for the organization to be given another grant. No wonder that in this situation monitoring becomes a merely symbolic counting of newspaper coverage or a head count of attendance at the organization's activities.[5]

Beyond these considerations, inescapably, there will always be the question of rationing scarce resources between competing demands and objectives – which will mean that you'll need to have developed a clear sense of priorities as between your primary and your subsidiary objectives, so that you can be clear which objectives and demands must be allowed to over-rule others in case of conflict.

4. Organizational culture and motivation

Having spent rather a long time decrying the mistake of concentrating exclusively on 'means' rather than 'ends', it's necessary to say something about 'means'. Since many people spend a great deal of their time working, it's surprising that the radical movements as a whole have not taken more interest in the 'quality of work'. What we're thinking of here is not necessarily a negative definition of work in terms of 'terms and conditions' within a contract negotiated by a trade union, but how people actually feel about the work they do.

The good organization breeds a sense of responsibility or commitment in everyone who works in it, so that they can say 'our organization' rather than saying, 'Oh, that's not my job,' or 'That's nothing to do with me.' So, for instance, when a new problem arrives which doesn't necessarily fall within anyone's formal set of responsibilities, it doesn't become 'nobody's problem', but instead is viewed as 'our problem', to be dealt with.

This sense of responsibility can only arise where people share a common understanding of what the organization has agreed to try to do, even though they may not all personally give the same order of priority to these goals. A typical democratic organization may have, say, three broad sets of reasons for being attractive to those who work in them:

i)   External aims – campaigning, helping people, etc.

ii) Internal aims – working democratically, equality within

iii) The quality of work – informality, encouragement, etc.

Every organization has, or develops, its own culture. This may consist of:

* Its history and how those who work there understand it – this is why it may be important to discuss and argue the significance of what has happened to an organization. An organization without a collective history is an organization without a sense of identity, and may seem confused to 'outsiders'.

* The declared objectives and values of the organization and how they are understood (and perhaps even misunderstood) in different parts of the organization.

* The informal aspects of work that influence the 'quality of work'. How people get on with each other, the social life of the organization, etc.

While organizations within the radical world are generally strong in their possession of an organizational culture, it should not be forgotten that because theirs is an oppositional culture – one that goes against the prevailing values – they are especially prone to a form of cultural implosion. Energies which under happier, or less exhausted circumstances, are directed at changing the world can recoil back into the organization with an intensity that can be destructive. The history of radical organizations is full of ritual purges in which everything that is wrong with the world is fought out internally.

5. Flexibility and innovation
One of the difficulties faced by most forms of collective is the structural conservatism, or bias against action ('Oh, it'll have to be discussed at the meeting first . . .') they often create. If you have given an individual responsibility within an organization and he or she decides that the best course of action is 'X', is it really necessary that everyone must formally agree this at a meeting before the action can be carried out?

This difficulty can, perhaps, be best illustrated by looking at how certain radical/alternative organizations have viewed 'new technology'. Five years ago, any group discussing this issue would usually find themselves in almost unanimous agreement that 'new technology' was not something they wanted to consider. A variety of reasons were advanced, which included job losses, health hazards and so on. Two years ago, the discussion was far more evenly divided between those who claimed that 'new technology was useful for certain types of work' and those who were still implacably opposed to its introductrion in their organization. As this is being written, the GLC are funding the purchase of microcomputers for many groups in London, and a wide variety of organizations throughout the country see nothing unusual in their use. The question raised by this example is that if there are benefits to be derived from the introduction of 'new technology' into these organizations, why has it taken many of them five years to persuade themselves of those benefits? And what is the cost (in terms of lost opportunities) of failing to get the two- to five-year 'headstart' they could have had if the decision to move in this direction had not taken so long?

Any form of organization must have the flexibility to allow (and, indeed, positively encourage) innovation, so that the organization is capable of taking advantage of either political or commercial opportunities quickly. This can probably only happen if most people in the organization have a clear understanding of the 'ends' which the organization is trying to achieve. This understanding is often hampered by a conflation of 'ends' and 'means' where people begin to argue that the 'means' are the only successful 'guarantee' of the 'ends'. Unless you can agree the 'ends' and then allow yourself the maximum room for manoeuvre on the 'means' (within the limits set by your agreed principles), democratic organizations will generally be slower moving than hierarchical organizations (like the Conservative Party) or companies in the marketplace. The alternative to authoritarianism cannot be that only the full collective meeting has the authority to make a decision; in this context we find the idea of relative or accountable authority especially crucial. By this, we mean authority granted by the whole to a sub-group or an individual who then has the responsibility and power to make decisions within agreed limits, subject to periodic assessment of their performance by the whole group.

The idea of innovation is not just some buzz word borrowed from Thatcherite 'technospeak', but a recognition that every organization must actively search for more effective ways of carrying on its activities and, where appropriate, of producing better products or services. No amount of being 'right' or 'having the right politics' alone ensures the quality of practical activity. Every organization should encourage its workers and/or members to generate innovation at every level. And the vital role of innovation should be recognized and legitimized at the highest level of the organization, whether you are dealing with commercial products or social ideas.

Chapter VII

The political economy of the future?

Our argument so far has offered some account of the way in which a variety of organizations and projects have dealt with questions of self-management over the last decade. While we want to widen the focus in this concluding chapter, we hope to do so without disappearing into the all-too-familiar reaffirmation of abstract generalities. Our aim, instead, is to look forward from where we stand. Our position is informed by what we have been doing over the last 10 years, and it is from this perspective that we will now indicate the place which the particular concerns of this book find within a broader political framework.

Our activities at Comedia have been centred around means of distribution, access and exchange. This, quite logically, has led us to be interested in intermediary mechanisms such as the market. In a decade that was preoccupied with tracking down 'bias' and the effect of 'ideology' within the mass media, our concerns have also included a more prosaic and less popular project. We have put our effort into defining how people can achieve a greater degree of public expression – and not just through the BBC. We have been interested in the possible impact and distribution of, say, alternative newspapers or radio stations. We have tried to help open up the systems of distribution, so that a wider range of publications can move into a circulation broader than the familiar backyard or ghetto.

In other words, while we have no doubt that the mass media are indeed filled with 'Bad News', we have not wanted just to say so over and over again in increasingly elaborate terms. Our interest has lain increasingly in the development of public forums or spaces – however local, specialist or particular in focus – through which a wider social imagination can be developed. This is how we understand the challenge of translating 'theory' into 'practice'.

In this respect our interest has never been in defining socialism against the present as a kind of island in the sun which will be achieved, either as a perfect television image or as a realized and unitary state of society, in the future. As we see it socialism is inextricably interwoven with the *present* possibilities of democracy – with the deepening and extension of democracy in the here-and-now, and most definitely not with its mockery or dismissal as a mere 'bourgeois' sham. In this regard we follow Ferenc Fehér and Agnes

Heller in their definition of socialism as 'the radicalization of democracy.'[1]

If we are to take this idea of the radicalization of democracy seriously, then we must move beyond the varied impasses, not just of libertarianism as this book has described it, but of labourism as well. For a start we must widen the range of organizations which are considered to form a relevant part of the picture. If we look forward to a society in which there is a greater plurality of self-managed activity, we should surely recognize that this will not be regulated by one correct and over-riding view of the world, but by shared and democratically formulated political principles which allow for difference and choice. Many of the organizations which are likely to contribute to this plurality will indeed have a directly political ambition. Some will be cultural and others production-based. Some of them will be neither radical nor directly socialist in their self-understanding. From the viewpoint of a radically democratic politics, it should be clear that if an organization helps people define and fulfil their own needs and aspirations – as a voluntary association, for example – then it is to be counted as a gain rather than a mere irrelevance. This judgement should extend to a whole range of organizations – whether federative mutual aid networks or free-standing agencies in their own right – in the health, environmental and leisure areas, all of which should be treated with the degree of seriousness which has customarily been reserved for traditional labour-based organizations such as the trade unions. While a measure of respect has indeed been won recently for the organizations of the Women's Movement, there are still other areas of concern whose significance is not widely recognized. Thus, for example, in a society where ordinary people are increasingly treated as if they need a training course before they can get out of bed in the morning, there should certainly be a critical revaluation of the enormous and complex range of 'hobby' and leisure organizations which exist in places where the Manpower Services Commission doubtless only sees a void. More generally, the connections between the constitutionally independent organizations of the 'voluntary sector' and colonial state agencies like the Manpower Services Commission, should be recognized as a key area in which traditions of self-determination are at stake.

In sum, if an organization – be it productive, service-based or a mutual aid network – enables people to articulate and meet their needs free from domination, and if it does so without contravening other people's needs and rights, then it should be seen as a positive gain in the present, and not merely judged in terms of whether it will help bring an abstractly defined 'socialism' tomorrow. This has obvious bearing on the questions of effectiveness which we have already posed. Organizations of all kinds have to be succeeding and expanding their area of influence if together they are to establish a social imagination capable of countering the mean, self-centred and 'individualistic' ethos that presently masquerades as commonsense.

Clearing debris

Of course there is also opposition. Ground has to be won against opposed political interests. However, while we do not mean to underestimate this opposition, which is ranged against even the most modest radical initiative, we also need to be concerned with problems which are to be found much closer to home. As we have tried to figure out the terms of a practical democratic socialism, we have repeatedly found ourselves up against the received political wisdom of the left. In this concluding chapter, therefore, we will indicate how the possibilities for the existence of more autonomous and self-managed organizations of the sort we have described are hampered by the inadequacy of contemporary socialist thinking about (a) the state, (b) the polity and (c) the economy.

Before we can approach these issues, however, we should suggest that the problem is pervasively one of mismatch between socialist rhetoric and the actualities with which it must deal. This may be a problem of philosophical idealism in the thought of the left – of ideas (like the unitary 'proletariat' with its universal and general interest) that don't match reality, but it is also a problem of institutionalized memory and its relation to changing circumstances in the present. Zygmunt Bauman[2] has described this in terms of 'historical memory'. Just as the political culture of the early industrial labour movement referred back so forcefully to the pre-industrial craft world where the individual producer owned the product of his own labour, so the contemporary labour movement often seeks answers to new questions (like the new technology and its destruction of work) by falling back on the assumptions which guided the establishment of the welfare state (among which were included an assumption about full employment ...). While there can be no question of simply dispensing with historical memory, there are times when the reassuring rhetoric ('this great movement of ours', etc.) seems to mask not just ignorance but also a lack of interest in the real functioning and impact of institutions which, rightly or not, are often claimed as part of the socialist cause.

The state

A primary example of this is provided by the institutions of the welfare state. Let us take the case of council housing which, despite the socialist rhetoric of 'opposition to council house sales', etc., is frequently experienced by working-class tenants as bureaucratic, paternalistic and alienating. As Bea Campbell, among others, has written, those who live in the decaying urban estates, where it is hard to get repairs done by the council and where the consequences of unemployment concentrate, do not generally see themselves as residents of the New Kingdom. They are more likely to be left with a feeling that 'socialism' has gone wrong, and with a bitter feeling of helplessness and powerlessness. The rift between socialist rhetoric and popular experience will only widen if the real effects of social intervention on people's lives are treated as secondary or accidental.

It is a commonplace that the welfare state in Britain (as in other advanced capitalist societies) has entered a crisis of legitimacy.[3] The 'post-war settlement' between the competing political economic and social interests in society was based on a Keynesian economic policy designed to even out the economic disequilibria created by the unfettered capitalist market. The near eradication of unemployment in the post-war period was only made possible through social engineering and public intervention in an expanding economy. With an ever-growing cake, conflicts could be bought off or obscured. In the scarcity of recent years, however, the limits of social engineering become apparent. Much has been written on the crisis of the welfare state and we will only stress three aspects of the situation.

As the post-war state increasingly colonized everyday life, it simultaneously interfered with traditional forms of self-regulation and social security. Thus, for example, while the family remains the main agent of socialization, its traditional functions have been increasingly taken over by the state – education, childcare, housing, etc. This is a process which certainly involves gains (for example, the possibility of going out to work for some women), but it is often experienced in an overwhelmingly negative register – the destruction of old forms of self-determination that occur when these areas of life are penetrated by procedures which follow the bureaucratic and administrative rationality of welfare state provision. As it has taken on an expanded role, the state has become significantly distant from the people to whom it is nominally accountable. The technocrats, planners, civil servants and professionals employed by the state operate in a world of their own, governed by procedures and rules in which only 'experts' and 'bureaucrats' are competent. In the course of the development of the welfare state, one area has been wholly neglected.

The state has extended its sphere of influence without developing the genuinely democratic mechanisms whereby those whose lives it affects can control it. Thousands of crumbling and socially dangerous tower blocks now stand as symbols of people's just disillusion with state 'development' of this sort. How ironic, indeed, that when Labour borough councils try to redress this imbalance by establishing local neighbourhood offices, it should be the bureaucrats and experts who invoke the union to prevent any progress in this direction...

Despite all the recent expansion, of the state, Britain has remained as unequal a society as ever – and not just in terms of wealth distribution. Through the fifties' and sixties' inequality was simply alleviated or bought off by the fact that the overall size of the cake was expanding. By the mid-seventies and the end of the post-war boom, there was far less economic possibility. Broadly speaking, the state response to this involved resisting such wage demands as it could (especially within the public sector) and acceding only when it was strategically necessary (as in the miners' strike of 1972). The state became increasingly busy as manager of crisis after crisis. In its corporatist form, the state was compelled to buy off the demands that came accompanied with the largest threats of disruption. With the technological basis of production undergoing massive transformation, there was no longer the promise of full employment to buy off dissatisfaction and, as a consequence, what Bauman calls 'new victims' have appeared. These are groups of people who lack powerful representation near or within the state. Their bargaining power – at least through legitimate channels – is slight, and their cause is not easily or organically expressed in the established institutions and framework of the labour movement. Among these groups are the unemployed, the sick and elderly who are dependent on public health provision, single parents, ethnic minorities, the low paid and a lot of women.

The post-war expansion of the state was due not simply to the triumph of 'socialism', but to the altogether more prosaic fact that the capitalist market did not in itself produce the social infrastructure on which it depends. The welfare state developed as an agent of *commodification* – ensuring that the capital-labour relation entered the 'free market' intact and fit for business. Thus, the state had to intervene in housing, health, transport and education on the one hand, while it also had to shelter new economic initiatives from the side of capital on the other. It has mediated between social needs and demands and the interests of capital over issues like pollution, and it has sought to create, by means of various financial incentives, the environment in which new firms could develop – firms which wouldn't stand a chance if the market dictated on its own terms. The demands of commodification are massive, as are their financial costs, and it is not at all surprising that – quite apart from problems of legitimacy – this expansion of state activity should also have led into what is known as 'the fiscal crisis of the state'. The essential point – one to which Thatcher (for all her rhetoric of 'rolling back the frontiers of the state') has no adequate answer – is not whether the state is corporatist or not. As the Thatcher government has discovered, even an anti-corporatist state will have to deal (or be seen not to deal) with the massive costs of commodifying and also legitimizing the supposedly 'free' market. You can hive off the profitable bits, decrease the welfare functions, centralize authority, pour money into police and surveillance; you can throw in a few national spectacles to replace other forms of social security – but at the end of the day a crude truth remains. The welfare state stands to the 'free' market rather as the National Trust stands to numerous other historical relics. Unless that relic is constantly guarded and preserved, the whole thing is going to start falling apart.

In short, the welfare state has created both new problems and new demands. Simply extending the existing services of the welfare state would be to institutionalize the problems still further, rather than to solve them. In other words, the politics of the welfare state demand that the very framework itself be changed, so that people are able to formulate their needs, determine the priorities which should govern statutory activity and judge for themselves what is best for them. As for the 'new victims', as Bauman describes them, any genuine understanding of how their victimization has come about would surely indicate the need not just for change in the state, but for a diversity of new organizations to be developed around their interests. Doubtless these people will make their own way, but their cause will hardly be helped if the established labour movement fails to understand the necessity for developments of this sort.

The polity

(a) Radical democracy

If socialism is about the 'radicalization of democracy', then the dismissal of 'bourgeois democracy' as a mere sham must rate as high folly. This is not to say that one accepts liberal definitions of democracy as they are, or that democracy exists in an achieved form. A thoroughly limited definition of democracy is constantly being invoked to justify capitalist development and we have already indicated our negative view of the simulated democracy (CBI and

TUC leaders meeting in small rooms, carefully stage-managed public enquiries . . .) of the corporatist state. Similarly, we do not talk about democracy only to join in the national fetishization of the parliamentary system.

But if democracy has been heavily contested in its development there is, nevertheless, a long tradition of democratic activism which, as Tony Benn often stresses, goes back ' behind' Marx. Samuel Smiles' notion of 'self-help' may have been appropriated within Thatcher's style of neo-Conservatism, but this doesn't mean that we can afford to ignore the positive republican elements in the bourgeois democratic tradition – a tradition which stresses (in an admittedly partial form) the value of self-determination and freedom and which, in its definition of citizenship, emphasizes the importance of free public activity over private egoism.

The existence of this republican tradition doesn't provide ready-made answers. Democracy is a dynamic, and it doesn't consist of a static set of tricks – the techniques of an enlightened social engineering. We can't simply resurrect the demands of the 19th century democratic movements (as Tony Benn seems to do in his references to Chartism), as if they were appropriate to the changed circumstances of our own time. If we took this approach we would simply be mirroring the Conservative endeavour to enlist history as an already completed national 'past' which demands appropriate reverence from the present. Rather than picking over the past in this way, we need to find the policies and forms of political organization through which the *contemporary* radicalization of democracy can occur. Thus, for example, the contemporary equivalent of the Chartist demand for an annually elected Parliament may well be found in the demand for proportional representation.

(b) Representation

What we have at the moment is a limited and symbolic democracy that does not fulfil its promises: it only allows a five-yearly ballot to a limited range of institutions, and it only expresses the views of a largely white, middle-class set of representatives. We need an extension of public involvement and a public definition of needs which moves through a wider range of representative forums and institutions.

Whilst the question of democracy cannot be limited exclusively to matters of representation, in particular parliamentary representation, these questions do need to be addressed. While the parliamentary system is imbued with a sacrosanct aura as part of the national heritage, the system that all true Brits must take for granted, there is an obvious disparity between the representational needs of our complex and differentiated society and the existing Westminster system.

While, in our view, the introduction of a system of proportional representation may indeed offer a valuable extension of democracy, the fact remains that if we want to meet the claims for representation of all groups who feel excluded, we cannot persist with the merely geographic system of representation by constituency. If the state needs to be opened to users, then the system of representation itself needs to be opened up to groups and interests currently excluded from the system.

There is often talk about abolishing the House of Lords, but perhaps the idea of a bi-cameral house points us in a better direction. The functional areas of social life could be represented in this second chamber, which might be made up of people representing, say, education, transport, health, environment, the nationalized industries, etc. In this way expertise could inform political decision-making and at the same time be drawn into public accountability, rather than always being located elsewhere – in the civil service, in the Quangos, in the interest group organizations, which are usually unaccountable (and often incomprehensible) to the outside world.

(c) Democracy in one city: The Greater London Council

So far, although we have talked about the need for greater democracy and participation, we have not specified how we believe this can best be achieved. The examples which are often cited (Lucas Combine Committees, Meriden Coop, etc.) are usually quoted as examples without a framework, an untidy clutter of 'how things might be'.

The GLC under Ken Livingstone has often – and quite rightly – been quoted as an example of a new type of 'municipal socialism' and has recently had some opportunity to develop more practical experience in these areas. Among its achievements we would count not just the establishment of the Policy and Performance Review Committee to ensure that policies are translated into effective and efficient action but also the difficulties of democracy itself which the GLC has revealed. After all, if we don't have experience to learn from, we are in a poor position – and valuable experience is not always simply 'successful' . . . As a socialist local authority, the GLC has sought to become more democratic by opening its policy formulation and workings to a wider group of people. It has proceeded from the view that democracy should operate outside election time, and so has sought to hear and represent a wider range of voices with a greater regularity than the election process allows. To do this it has set up within County Hall, or funded externally, a wide range of bodies designed to represent the views of 'minorities' whose views have previously not been represented, or have been under-presented in the local government of London. These have in-cluded women, blacks, the Irish, the disabled, gays, and so on – precisely those 'new victims' of Bauman's description.

But these admirable attempts to create new forms and institutions of radical democracy have often run into significant difficulties. For example, the GLC Women's Committee is elected by a meeting of whoever turns up; a meeting that probably (optimistically) could only be as large as a few hundred women. It is from this narrow franchise that the Committee claims the political legitimacy to talk for 'all the women of London'. Lest this be thought to be too narrow a grouping, it co-opts representatives (who then have the power to vote) who, in turn, claim to be representative of some wider constituency – but who themselves are usually elected by a very small group of people, if indeed they are elected at all.

This is 'activist' democracy, whereby a small, often self-selecting, group claims to represent some wider group of people by virtue of their being active. The same problem faces the Labour Party over the issue of one-member, one-vote. You cannot seek to persuade people that you want a more democratic society and simultaneously restrict the franchise to only those activists who are able to attend particular meetings. Elective democracy has many faults but it, at least, consults all of the people who get to the polls once every five years.

'Activist' democracy also holds the seeds of its own downfall because it often cuts itself off from those who it most sincerely wants to represent.

' ... it's a mode of participation [the GLC Women's Committee] that is much more familiar to those with a history of political activism. Providing a crèche and a minibus will help Mrs Bloggs to get to the meetings but won't necessarily make her feel they are "for her", or enable her to express her views in a way that those fluent in the language and behaviour codes of political meetings can. These can be just as alien and arcane as the rituals of bureaucracy. Nor can it be assumed that Mrs Smith, because she's a feminist, represents Mrs Bloggs.'[4]

This problem, which should certainly be familiar to anyone with any experience of community work, is only likely to be aggravated if initiatives and projects are claimed as examples of radical democracy or 'popular planning' in practice *before* these problems of access and alienation have been properly thought through.

Our argument is not against the Women's Committee, or forums of this sort. Any movement into public formulation of policy is an advance on secrecy and 'clubland connections'. Indeed, the GLC committees should be thanked rather than criticized for making these difficulties visible. The primary question, as we see it, concerns representation. To claim properly to talk for and represent all the women of London, you would need to be elected by a majority of all the women of London. So you might have, say, a number of women councillors specifically selected to represent women, a further number to represent blacks, and so on. Although this proposition may sound – and indeed be – unlikely, it does have the virtue of forcing one to think about how the language and behaviour codes suitable for activist politicos will have to change if they are to enable the all-purpose Mrs Bloggs not just to vote for the views which claim to represent her 'true interests', but actively to formulate them.

Currently, councillors are elected on a geographical basis and thus may only partly be able to claim legitimacy to represent and thus talk on behalf of other non-geographical interest groups, like the elderly, the disabled, etc. However, there is indeed no reason in principle why geographical communities, as opposed to communities of interest, should provide the only basis for an electoral system.

While the GLC has followed this route around the interests of what are still often called 'minorities', the ideas could apply equally in functional areas like transport, housing and education. So, for instance, in the field of public transport one could develop forums which give people the chance to take part in designing the type of transport they wanted, and hold open and genuine discussions about the problems and limitations of public finance.

The local authority could sponsor the costs of a widely advertised election to the committee of Transport Users, which could have the services of a small number of paid researchers. Such a form of democracy could be favourably contrasted with the largely hidden process of selection which chooses the 'great and the good' to people the wide range of 'quangos' set up to perform similar 'oversight' roles: it would also contrast refreshingly with the toothless and merely symbolic existence of the various Nationalized Industry Consultative Committees.

It would surely be healthy to create a range of legitimate 'user' bodies which could criticize, suggest improvements and shape policy for a wide range of public services. These bodies might find themselves in conflict with trade unions as the interests of those 'users' and workers in the public sector do not necessarily coincide. But such conflicts would help to revive and add meaning to the debates which need to take place about public service; how we treat those workers who we, after all, are responsible for employing to provide services, and how those workers can best provide a public service which will be remembered for its helpfulness and effectiveness.

In all these cases a key question will concern the resolution of inevitable conflicts of interest, between workers producing services and those who use them (and, indeed, between the interests of the same person in their different roles). Nove gives the simple example of it being in the interest of train drivers not to have to run late-night services – but it being in the interest of their users that they should exist.[5] The problem here, as always, will be how to develop mechanisms (extra payments or early retirement credit for drivers willing to run such services?) to resolve such conflicts of interest – not to pretend that under 'socialism' such necessary conflicts of interest will disappear. Nor will it do to assume that, as socialists, we solve the problem by simply defending the workers' interests, as trades unionists. The problem with this position is that it reduces the citizen to his or her capacity as a worker, and fails to provide any sensible way of conceiving of, and organizing, the citizens' interests in their non-work capacities – e.g., as users of services provided by other workers. The more radicalized the democracy, the more views and desires will enter the arena and the more disputation, negotiation and healthy argument there will be. But who was it that wanted a quiet life? Isn't political quiet also rather deathly from the viewpoint of democracy?

The economy

(a) From abundance to scarcity

Whether we are dealing with capitalism or socialism, we have to accept that we are dealing with finite resources. Because of this we have to make choices about what our priorities are going to be, since we are unlikely to have the resources to do everything immediately. As Nye Bevan once put it, 'Socialism is all about priorities.' Indeed, a strong argument can be made that one of the key reasons for the Labour Party's electoral failure in 1983 was that it presented an uncosted 'maximalist' programme, simply promising more of everything to everybody, without any clear definition of the cost of its various promises.

We also believe that the present socialist fixation with the provision of social welfare, without asking how the resources to provide that welfare are to be generated, comes from a simplistic view that the state somehow has wealth 'locked in', wealth that just needs to be tapped; or even that socialism can be built, without problems, out of the resources 'saved' once capitalist 'wastages' (e.g., advertising, in some arguments) have been abolished.

Our view is that – even after the City and its export of capital from Britain has been curbed – the problem of wealth creation is bound to remain central in importance. In this connection we would suggest that a major shift has to be made from an exclusive emphasis on changing the rules and structure of the distributive game via traditional political activity (aimed at 'capturing' the state and thus control over resources) to an approach that sees the setting up of alternative structures of economic activity, which are autonomous from the State, as of at least equal importance. This strategy is then, focused on developing the existing political economy of the radical movements.

Our thinking in this area involves a set of assumptions about how radical change can occur and about the kind of society we would like to live in. We will now outline the framework within which our thinking occurs.

(b) Consumers, users and choices

At the core of the ideas we're developing here is the notion that, as citizens, we are all *users* of goods and services, both in the public and private sectors, and that there is a real need to provide real *choices* in both sectors. We avoid the word 'consumer' as a degraded term which implies that a person is merely the sum of his or her buying decisions. In our understanding 'user' implies a much wider and more complex set of relationships, not all of them necessarily expressed in 'buying' decisions.

The term *users* also enables us to look pragmatically at the function of the market as a 'feedback mechanism' – a mechanism that may in some ways be *more* equitable than centrally planned state control, and more efficient than a system in which we will all vote on the exact needs of our supermarket shopping basket in some popular forum. No system of 'top-down' planning or periodic consumer vote can substitute for the direct expression of what we use – whether that be what goods we buy or what services we use. This is what socialist economists refer to as 'voting with the rouble' and it goes some way towards explaining why some Eastern Bloc economies are presently experimenting with ways of introducing a 'market' element into their planned economies.

Past attempts

Past attempts to control matters like those of taste – whether for economic or political reasons – have proved inadequate. Often attempts to restrict choice, through legislation or taxation, serve only to increase opposition to this type of paternalistic intervention. Thus, for example, the Wilson government's first response to Radio Caroline was to try to close down the private radio stations rather than to contemplate the un-Reithian option of providing a rock music station via public service broadcasting. Eventually popular pressure forced it to do just that, and Radio One was launched.

An earlier example can be found in the tangles the Attlee Government got itself into with rationing where, for perfectly understandable economic reasons, it tried to control style and eating habits. Its campaign to persuade women to wear short skirts to conserve material for other uses only accelerated the pace at which women wanted longer dresses. Likewise, the Minister of Food's wish to persuade people to eat a strange fish called Snoek (even inventing a recipe for Snoek Piquant) came to absolutely nothing.[6] Outside of war and national emergency, you cannot gain popular support for dictating diet and dress from above, and even in those circumstances it's a difficult road to follow.

In this connection it is useful to think of the two-way role of the market mechanism. In many areas where the state does not wish to be hamfistedly telling people to wear this or to eat this or that (even if it's for their own good), it *could* encourage autonomous enterprise to launch new products (say to provide elements of a healthier diet) or other new services. The enterprise would clearly need to make a profit from its activities, but could receive financial encouragement in a variety of different ways to carry out social objectives.

As a feedback mechanism the market works differently for the private and public sectors. If consumers stop buying a particular type of food, then the decline in profit means that its producers have to think about its quality or reflect that tastes have changed and produce something else. The impact is obvious in the private sector, but in a more obscured way users make the same sort of choices about public services. Users choose to have their children in certain hospitals because those hospitals are more open-minded about new birthing methods, or they send their children to particular schools because they are happier with the education provided there. All these choices which will be made within the public sector (leaving aside the prerogative of the wealthy to buy into other choices in the private sector) might be described as simply the luxury of the well-informed middle-class. But surely the aim must be to expand the availability of this 'luxury' so that the widest possible range of users – instead of being progressively alienated from the services provided by the public sector – take an active part in saying rather loudly what they want. Only then will public services become more responsive to people's felt needs.

(c) Market mechanisms

For many people on the left the very notion of the 'market' is unacceptable. Identified with the capitalist marketplace, it is seen as an entirely manipulated space. However, the market holds certain positive features which have often been neglected by the left.

As Jim Tomlinson puts it:

'As far as consumer durable goods go markets are commonly a very effective means of satisfying consumer wants. Socialists commonly obscure this point by pointing to the alleged impact of advertising in shaping these wants. But advertising as an explanation of patterns of consumption is being asked to bear too much weight here: advertising cannot explain our attachment to motor cars, hi-fi and household gadgets. Consumers are not blank sheets of paper upon which anything can be written. There often seems to lurk behind socialist attacks on advertising a puritan distaste of consumption per se.

Of course markets have severe limitations as a means of satisfying consumer wants. But for many classes of goods it cannot easily be improved upon, indeed it may be prefererable to the non-market forms – queueing, patronage, etc. – so extensively experimented with in Eastern Europe.[7]

It is time to recognize that market mechanisms have progressive political possibilities as an index of social needs. The proviso is that one must bear in mind that the information that the market can give you on needs is always limited by existing distribution of wealth and income. What the market can tell you about is effective demand at a given price. Thus, needs which people have but cannot afford to meet at given prices, will be invisible. However, this limitation derives from the inequitable distribution of wealth under capitalism. To the extent that socialist development reduces the scale of that inequality, to that same extent this limitation on the 'feedback' that market mechanisms can give about needs is reduced.

For us, the market is not some mystical religion to which every area of life should correspond, but simply the most practical way of gaining information about the thousands of complex choices users make about goods and services. Clearly, in some areas, it ceases to have much value as a term and for these areas we do not pretend that it operates as a useful mechanism.

(d) Trades Unions and self-management

One cannot talk of socialist strategy without consideration of the role of the trade union movement. Weakened as the unions currently are (with current rates of unemployment, declining TU membership, etc.), they retain a key position in the Labour movement – even if the kinds of automatic links that used to be assumed between TU membership and Labour Party voting can no longer be held to be realistic.

However, it is as well to be clear about the role of trades unionism. The primary purpose of trades unions is to secure improvements and benefits for their members *within* existing political and economic structures. Here, as elsewhere, strength and limitations go hand-in-hand. Unions are justly defensive, justly concerned with the sometimes small but always immediate and important issues at hand. They are not necessarily involved in proliferating new kinds of organizational structures and activity – or with designing possible regimes to replace the hierarchical order of the capitalist enterprise or the public sector bureaucracy. Indeed, many unions are hamstrung by bureaucratic ways of organizing their activities, and by their productivist, male-orientated definition of collective interests. While there is, indeed, innovation within the union world, there are also substantial problems in getting beyond the style of defensive negotiation. Thus, for every Vickers or Lucas plan, there are many possibilities or initiatives which have been lost – like KME, the largest of the so-called Benn Co-ops, where the endeavour to derive an acceptable and working form of management from within the traditions of shop-floor culture (and other pressures not withstanding) finally came to nothing.

The last 15 years or so have seen the uneasy growth of a new development – self-managed enterprises and coops of various kinds, where some moves have been made beyond the notion of trades unionism as simply a set of defensive institutions serving workers' interests within the capitalist firm, towards the development of new forms of enterprise altogether. Vickers and Lucas Aerospace workers' plans, the Mondragon cooperatives, a few self-managed enterprises in Yugoslavia – these are (or have been) among the sacred names. Studied and lionized for their indisputable interest and value, such experiments have also been mythologized precisely because they are so rare. Indeed, there is such a weight of hope and ambition for them to support that the load-bearing capacity of these particular cases inevitably comes into question.

If we are to get beyond the mythologization we should, perhaps, start by asking how big the 'cooperative market' actually is. Once you take away the consumer co-ops (CWS, etc.) the 'rescues' (KME, *Scottish Daily News*) and the endowed co-ops (J. Lewis, Scott Bader), what are you left with? A few thousand producer coops, as Tony Eccles has estimated (see below). If cooperative working is as 'beneficial' as its protagonists claim (and as we are happy to accept) why has there been so much failure after 150 years? Why are there still so few co-ops? The sad answer is the resistance to the cooperative movement from all power bases – *including* the Trade Union movement and (until very recently) the Labour Party. In fact, the growth of the co-op economy may in some respects constitute a major threat to the Trade Union movement. Certainly ideas of worker-participation or of workers' cooperatives have met with intense suspicion from a defensive and sectional Trade Union movement.

The saddest thing, perhaps, has been the kind of situation described by Tony Eccles, where the workers in cooperatives such as KME or Third Sector have simply taken traditional trade union attitudes and practices into these new enterprises, and failed to recognize that they are inadequate and inappropriate in such different circumstances.[8] In KME, the shop stewards, who effectively had to take on a managerial role within the enterprise, seem to have refused to recognize this aspect of their role and spent a lot of time and energy trying to find a management to fight.

(e) Forms of ownership

Despite the talk of Britain's decline, we believe that the productive potential of our society is still very much untapped. It will probably remain so unless we see the development of a politically principled system of economic pluralism with a corresponding set of forums of political representation. By this we mean that, while ownership of key sections of the means of production would be *socialized* and in some cases run as nationalized industries, other sections of the economy may run on different principles. This system would produce a range of different types of goods and services and would not seek to use direct state intervention to curtail the range of goods and services provided, save in exceptional circumstances.

A scenario of this sort is spelt out in more detail by Alex Nove, who envisages a socialist economy comprised of a combination of centralized state corporations, socialized enterprise co-ops, small-scale private enterprise and individual tradespeople. For our part, we believe that Nove has come as close as anyone to sketching out the details of an efficient, democratic and desirable socialism. His work provides a good basis for the development of a popular socialist programme – a socialism which maintains the notion of user/con-sumer choice as an essential element in that programme. This emphasis on choice is essential if we are to create a dynamic economy which is capable of generating further social changes and innovations in production. This pluralism guarantees a range of different forms of ownership (including a limited private sector) which it will seek to make as effective and efficient as possible, so as to provide wealth for the public sector and the best goods and services for the people.

(f) Social markets – the politically defined economy

We think in terms of 'social' markets primarily because this perspective allows objectives and needs to be politically established. This is not monetarism with a human face.

If the relationship between the market and social needs is to be redefined, an attempt must be made to introduce some idea of performance criteria into areas of demand that both financially and politically may have no direct profitability. This demands that one answers some of the quantitative questions conventionally asked about a commercial market.

If we take the health service as an example, we can outline what this might mean. Since its creation, successive governments have poured increasingly large sums into the health service. As more money has gone in, so expectations have risen. Even people on the left have begun to ask whether this might not be a black hole into which you could throw almost limitless amounts of money. Doctors want better and more advanced equipment. Nurses and ancillaries want, and indeed need, more pay. And patients want more health care. The technological fix of current health care and the economic logic associated with it will mean that the costs will grow and grow. Demands for making the service more efficient will increase. Socialists obviously need a way of defining the social market for health care. We need to ask questions like: How many heart cases are there, and what does it cost to treat them in each area? Why is it more costly in one area? Is a heart transplant 'cost-effective' by this yardstick? What would be the cost-effectiveness of other forms of treatment? Would it not be better to spend resources on preventative medicine? Are not the alternative medicines more cost-effective ways of treatment? Does not the present system lead to centralized forms of health care? What impact could health education have on all this? To what extent are 'total institutions' needed and valuable, and where does 'community care' become cheap rhetoric? One has to produce some yardstick of efficiency and some evidence of demand to have any chance of controlling spending on social need in terms of political priorities. This perspective makes explicit what the possibilities are with a given set of resources. Can one borough produce a cheaper council house than the next? And if so, why?

We cannot assume that in the world of the 'socialist utopia' we would have enough money to buy our way out of all social problems. More houses? Build until there's no more demand. Hospitals? Build as many as are needed. And so on. Every time one confronts the problem – of producing for needs, not profits – one is dealing with finite resources. The term social markets doesn't imply there are objective criteria – the choices made will necessarily be political. But when you are able to define and quantify the needs which you are trying to satisfy, you can more easily draw up your priorities. With properly spelt-out priorities, there will be less disappointment from unkept promises.

A social definition of markets would also help create the incentive to be productive and innovative, since there is a competitive element which allows comparisons to be made about what is working (or not) and what is, or isn't, cost effective. But, equally, the definition of what is cost-effective is broader than in traditional capitalism because it includes social and political criteria.

(g) Gramscian economics

A political strategy of the sort we are arguing for could help to develop a sound and growing economic infrastructure for the radical movements which will sustain them in their activity, with the least possible degree of dependence on the state or other external funding agencies and, thus, with the greatest possible degree of genuine autonomy.

In theoretical terms, such a strategy is related to Gramsci's notion of a long-term 'war of position', through which a subordinate culture gradually strengthens itself and spreads its sphere of influence – to the point at which it achieves hegemony as the 'common sense' of the culture.

For Gramsci (and even more in subsequent discussion of his work), this perspective operated mainly at the level of ideology – but a comparable way of thinking needs to be applied to the development of the economic sphere as well. The ready availability of various forms of state grants (e.g., to subsidize various forms of 'independent' cultural work) over the last few years, is one of the reasons why it has been possible for people to neglect the need to develop a truly independent economic base for this culture. In the past, where the question of the need for such a material base for this kind of cultural strategy has been considered at all, it has been addressed solely as a problem of gaining political control of various state institutions which can then be mobilized in support of this kind of cultural work. However, it is clear that the period in which this kind of strategy alone was viable (where this kind of cultural work could be indefinitely subsidized by the state) is drawing to a close.

In this context we believe that it is vital to develop a strategy for the 'independent' (or, more accurately, 'state-dependent') sector, one which will enable it to secure its own economic infrastructure. This is the necessary economic underpinning to a Gramscian political strategy – whereby the subordinate culture can develop the economic base it needs to sustain itself on the long road to hegemony.

This strategy may well be related to the developing 'alternative' or 'counter-cultures' which have been quoted in political debate at various points since the early 1970s. The main problem, in the past, has of course been that these 'alternative' or 'counter-cultural' projects have tended to remain marginalized – only operating in the margins left by the major commercial companies, and making no inroads into the mainstream markets. Moreover, these projects have usually been dependent both on state subsidies of one form or another and, as we have described, on the willingness of those working in them to exploit their own labour to a high degree. The combination of these two forms of dependency makes these projects fundamentally unstable and the vast majority of them have a short life-span (two to seven years). However, these 'alternative' projects serve a vital function. For instance, in the cultural sphere, such projects often operate as the 'greenhouses' in which new cultural forms (e.g., feminist publishing; new wave music; art cinema) first develop. They will give opportunities to new producers who the commercial companies regard as too high a risk. Unfortunately, this function is then usually economically exploited by the major commercial companies: at the point at which the 'alternatives' have produced something which has the chance of commercial viability, the 'majors' move in and 'sign up' the producers, who then leave the sector (which cannot meet their ambitions for wider distribution, marketing, etc.).

By this means the 'alternative' sector (cf. the 'independent' music business) continually functions as a kind of unpaid 'Research and Development' department for the major commercial companies – who then siphon off the 'best', thus continually draining the sector of those elements which could otherwise provide the financial return which would strengthen its own development. Thus, the network of 'alternative' projects fails, on the whole, to build any secure, long-term economic foundation for itself.

The existing radical political economy is small and consists of a very limited number of productive enterprises covering areas such as wholefoods (where their success has had a major impact on food retailing); publishing, printed and related media activities; bookshops; film and video workshops; and so on. But many of the groups and projects have not thought in strategic terms about the economic and political power at their disposal, and so far have missed the opportunities of mobilizing that power in concert. They have at their disposal a number of strategic assets – these include the consumer-based cooperative supermarket chain, the "Co-op", the purchasing power of certain Labour-controlled councils, the investment funds of trades unions, etc., and with these they could greatly enlarge their sphere of influence if they had a more developed view of what could be possible.

Without an extension of the radical political economy, their marginality becomes a self-fulfilling prophecy. Because the sector is small and unable to generate enough surplus to pay people who work in it, it will constantly be losing its best talents to capitalism. Because working in the radical political economy is low-paid and requires an idealistic commitment over and above material considerations, in the long term it can only sustain employment for those who are young, single, without major financial commitments, or extremely prin-cipled, to the point of being prepared to engage in radical forms of self-exploitation. Others, who do not fall within these categories, are under strong pressure to work in traditional capitalist enterprises or various parts of the state at local or national level.

We need to create a political economy of the radical movements; a structure which can be measured by the extent to which the economic units within that economy can provide a self-sufficient alternative economic system for those that work in it, whether they have prefigurative forms of organization, such as cooperatives, or are producers of radical products or services with more traditional forms of organization. This economy should be capable of providing a range of goods and services that makes as wide an impact on the world outside the political ghettoes as is possible.

As this activity takes place in a sea of capitalism, it naturally involves all kinds of relations with that system. (These can range from needing an overdraft for your enterprise at the bank, to having to rent a photocopier from IBM.) But, as in political warfare, the strategies and tactics of these relationships have to be assessed in terms of how far they allow us to retain economic autonomy whilst extracting the maximum possible political advantage.

By autonomy, we mean the degree to which these economic units can survive commercially, and at the same time provide a decent standard of living for their employees – by generating sufficient sales of those products/services which they define as socially or politically useful. Autonomy also means the degree to which these autonomous economic units can intertrade with other similar units and in so doing can extract themselves from the prerogatives and priorities of the dominant capitalist system. If state funding can be used to facilitate and establish this independence, then so much the better. But for many projects, given the current situation, there won't be any form of life at all if there isn't life *after* the age of grant applications.

Notes

Chapter I: History and ideology

1. See, for example, Stuart Hall, 'The Great Moving Right Show' in *The Politics of Thatcherism*, London: Lawrence and Wishart, 1983, pp. 19–39. Also the exchange between Hall and Tony Benn in *Marxism Today*, January, 1985.
2. Ferenc Fehér and Agnes Heller, 'Equality Reconsidered', *Thesis Eleven*, No. 3, 1981, p. 29.
3. Lyn Segal, 'A Local Experience', in S. Rowbotham *et al.*, *Beyond the Fragments*, Merlin Press, 1979.
4. Sheila Rowbotham, 'The Women's Movement & Organising for Socialism', Rowbotham *et al.*, *op. cit.*
5. Sheila Rowbotham, *op. cit.*, p. 30.
6. Richard Seyd, 'The Theatre of Red Ladder', *New Edinburgh Review*, No. 30, August, 1975.

Chapter II: A case-study in failure

1. From an early internal document of the Leveller's planning group. Other quoted passages likewise.

Chapter III: Living in the market

1. See Martin J. Wiener, *English Culture and the Decline of the Industrial Spirit*, 1850–1980, Cambridge University Press, 1981.
2. Mark Lloyd, unpublished paper on 'The East End News Experience'.

Chapter IV: The collective decides

1. 'Newsreel, five years on', *Wedge* 3, Winter, 1978.
2. Mike Davis *et al.*, *Go Local to Survive; decentralisation in Local Government*, Labour Coordinating Committee, 1984, p. 25.
3. 'Newsreel, five years on', *Wedge* 3, Winter, 1978.

Chapter V: Looking a management with a jaundiced eye

1. An accessible survey of this more theoretical tradition is to be found in Michael Rose, *Industrial Behaviour; theoretical development since Taylor*, Penguin, 1978.
2. It is significant in this connection that many senior managers have expressed doubts about the Tebbit approach to the unions – one that consists of legislating them into the ground. Unions are part of the fabric of organizational management by now, but as many of these managers also suggest, there may well be a backlash if you play class struggle too actively. Of course the 'disarray' of the unions – partly caused by new legislation – is still useful. It provides an opportunity to 'build bridges' of a new sort. See Francis Kinsman, *The New Agenda*, London, Spencer Stuart Management Consultants, 1983, p. 65.
3. See John Adair, *Training for Leadership*, London, Macdonald and Jane's, 1968. Such myths of leadership are well debunked in the opening chapter of Pierre Guillet de Monthoux's quirky *Action and Existence; Anarchism for business administration*, John Wiley and Sons, 1983.
4. In the last few years the Industrial Society has recognized the limitations of 'man-management' and started to run development courses – based on the same set of ideas – for women in management.
5. Edwin P. Smith, 'The ACL Course, in John Adair, *Action-Centred Leadership*, Farnborough, Gower, 1973, pp. 29–30.
6. Thomas Peters and Robert Waterman, Junior, *In Search of Excellence; Lessons from America's Best-run Companies*, New York, Harper and Row, 1982.

7. Oral History Associates are based in San Francisco and advertise themselves as providing 'A unique way to utilise the past for the future'. As their leaflet says, 'informed employees are more productive. Your company story is a vital source for such information.'

8. Armand Mattelart, *Multinational Corporations and the Control of Culture*, Harvester Press, 1979.

9. We draw these arguments from Jim Tomlinson's excellent [sic] *The Unequal Struggle? British Socialism and the Capitalist Enterprise*, Methuen, 1982.

10. This sort of absolutist refusal works on the assumption that 'contemporary technique is well and truly capitalistic... modelled upon specifically capitalist objectives... Consequently as long as this type of technique prevails, it is impossible to speak of self-management' Cornelius Castoriadis, Interview in *Thesis Eleven*, No. 8, 1984, p. 128. The trouble is that from here there are only the vaguest indications of what authentic self-management might actually look like.

Chapter VI: Where do we go from here?

1. Charles Handy, 'Volorgs', in *The Management Committees Issue*, MDU Bulletin No. 5, June, 1985.

2. Des Wilson, in an interview published in *Voluntary Action*, 1985.

3. Bruce Kokopeli and George Lakey, *Leadership for Change – Towards a feminist model*, New Society Publishers, Philadelphia, pp. 6–7. A more organically feminist enquiry (i.e., one conducted by women!) into questions of management is now going on throughout the country. There are also an increasing number of feminist management consultancies – like Synergy or Counterpoint, on which information is available from the Management Development Unit of the NCVO at 26 Bedford Square, London WC1. Tel: 01-636-4066.

4. Ken Edwards, 'Collective Working in a Small Non-Statutory Organisation', in *MDU Bulletin* No. 4/5, July, 1984.

5. We draw here on Alvin Gouldner's very interesting article on 'The Secrets of Organizations', *Social Welfare Forum*, New York, 1963, pp. 163–77. A summary of this article's main points appears in *MDU Bulletin*, No. 6, October, 1985.

Chapter VII: The political economy of the future?

1. Ferenc Fehér and Agnes Heller have outlined this definition of socialism in a number of places. See, for example, their essay 'Class, Modernity, Democracy', in *Theory and Society*, 12, 1983. See, also, Patrick Wright's interview with Agnes Heller, 'A Socialist in Exile', *New Socialist*, 29, July/August, 1985.

2. Zygmunt Bauman, *Memories of Class: the pre-history and after-life of class*, London, R.K.P., 1982.

3. This perspective on the state is influenced both by Bauman (see above) and Claus Offe – see Claus Offe, *Contradictions of the Welfare State*, London, Hutchinson, 1984.

4. From Frankie Rickford's article, 'Love, the media and the GLC', *New Statesman*, 21/28, December, 1984. See, also, Ali Mantle's pamphlet, *Popular Planning – Not in Practice: confessions of a community worker*, Greenwich Employment Resource Unit, London, 1985, which raises a number of similar issues about the gaps between the theory and practice of 'participation'.

5. Alec Nove, *The Economics of Feasible Socialism*, Allen & Unwin, 1983.

6. See Michael Sissons and Philip French (Eds.), *The Age of Austerity, 1945–51*, London, Penguin, 1967.

7. Jim Tomlinson, *The Unequal Struggle*, Methuen, 1982.

8. Tony Eccles, *Under New Management: the story of Britain's largest worker co-operative – its success and failures*, London, Pan, 1981.

Other titles from Comedia

No. 6   **THE REPUBLIC OF LETTERS — WORKING-class writing and local publishing** edited by David Morley and Ken Worpole
£3.95 paperback, £8.50 hardback

No. 5   **NEWS LTD — Why you can't read all about it** by Brian Whitaker
£3.95 paperback, £9.50 hardback

No. 4   **ROLLING OUR OWN — Women as printers, publishers and distributors** by Eileen Cadman, Gail Chester, Agnes Pivot
£2.25 paperback only

No. 3   **THE OTHER SECRET SERVICE — Press distribution and press censorship** by Liz Cooper, Charles Landry and Dave Berry
£1.20, paperback only

No. 2   **WHERE IS THE OTHER NEWS — The news trade and the radical press** by Dave Berry, Liz Cooper and Charles Landry
£2.75 paperback only

No. 1   **HERE IS THE OTHER NEWS — Challenges to the local commercial press** by Crispin Aubrey, Charles Landry and David Morley
£2.75 paperback only

Organizations and Democracy Series

No. 1   **WHAT A WAY TO RUN A RAILROAD — an analysis of radical failure** by Charles Landry, David Morley, Russell Southwood and Patrick Wright
£2.50 paperback only

No. 2   **ORGANIZING AROUND ENTHUSIASMS: Patterns of Mutual Aid in Leisure** by Jeff Bishop and Paul Hoggett
£5.95 paperback only

No. 3   **BAD SOLUTIONS TO GOOD PROBLEMS: The Practice of Organizational Change** by Liam Walsh
£3.95, paperback only, Spring 1986